Bloom's Modern Critical Interpretations

Joseph Conrad's
Heart of Darkness
New Edition

Edited and with an introduction by
Harold Bloom
Sterling Professor of the Humanities
Yale University

BLOOM'S
LITERARY CRITICISM
An imprint of Infobase Publishing

Bloom's Modern Critical Interpretations: Heart of Darkness—New Edition

Copyright © 2008 Infobase Publishing

Introduction © 2008 by Harold Bloom

Bloom's Literary Criticism
An imprint of Infobase Publishing
132 West 31st Street
New York NY 10001

Library of Congress Cataloging-in-Publication Data
Joseph Conrad's Heart of darkness / edited and with an introduction by Harold Bloom.
—New ed.
    p. cm.— (Modern critical interpretations)
  Rev. ed. of: 1987.
  Includes bibliographical references and index.
  ISBN 978-0-7910-9825-7 (hardcover)
  1. Conrad, Joseph, 1857–1924. Heart of darkness. 2. Psychological fiction, English—History and criticism. 3. Africa—In literature. I. Bloom, Harold.
  PR6005.O4H477 2008
  823'.912—dc22
                                    2007051300

Bloom's Literary Criticism books are available at special discounts when purchased in bulk quantities for businesses, associations, institutions, or sales promotions. Please call our Special Sales Department in New York at (212) 967-8800 or (800) 322-8755.

You can find Bloom's Literary Criticism on the World Wide Web at
http://www.chelseahouse.com

Contributing Editor: Pamela Loos
Cover designed by Takeshi Takahashi
Cover photo Stepffen Foerster Photography/Shutterstock.com
Printed in the United States of America
Bang EJB 10 9 8 7 6 5 4 3 2 1

This book is printed on acid-free paper.

All links and Web addresses were checked and verified to be correct at the time of publication. Because of the dynamic nature of the Web, some addresses and links may have changed since publication and may no longer be valid.

Contents

Editor's Note

My Introduction judges *Heart of Darkness* to be obscurantist, since neither Marlow nor Conrad always seems to know what he is talking about.

The late Edward Said folds Conrad's short novel into a dogma of culture and imperialism, while Cedric Watts defends Conrad against political critics like Said.

The celebrated "white fog incident" is seen by John Peters as an emblem of the entire story, after which Pericles Lewis finds in Marlow Conrad's English version of himself.

Hans Ulrich Seeber studies images of voice in the book, while James Morgan meditates upon the grotesque Russian sailor.

Padmini Mongia makes a qualified defense of Conrad against Achebe's charge of "racism," after which Hillis Miller more strongly endorses the book, and Bernard Paris returns us to the iconic figure of Marlow.

HAROLD BLOOM

Introduction

I

In Conrad's "Youth" (1898), Marlow gives us a brilliant description of the sinking of the *Judea*:

> "Between the darkness of earth and heaven she was burning fiercely upon a disc of purple sea shot by the blood-red play of gleams; upon a disc of water glittering and sinister. A high, clear flame, an immense and lonely flame, ascended from the ocean, and from its summit the black smoke poured continuously at the sky. She burned furiously; mournful and imposing like a funeral pile kindled in the night, surrounded by the sea, watched over by the stars. A magnificent death had come like a grace, like a gift, like a reward to that old ship at the end of her laborious day. The surrender of her weary ghost to the keeper of the stars and sea was stirring like the sight of a glorious triumph. The masts fell just before daybreak, and for a moment there was a burst and turmoil of sparks that seemed to fill with flying fire the night patient and watchful, the vast night lying silent upon the sea. At daylight she was only a charred shell, floating still under a cloud of smoke and bearing a glowing mass of coal within."

"Then the oars were got out, and the boats forming in a line moved around her remains as if in procession—the longboat leading. As we pulled across her stern a slim dart of fire shot out viciously at us, and suddenly she went down, head first, in a great hiss of steam. The unconsumed stern was the last to sink; but the paint had gone, had cracked, had peeled off, and there were no letters, there was no word, no stubborn device that was like her soul, to flash at the rising sun her creed and her name."

The apocalyptic vividness is enhanced by the visual namelessness of the "unconsumed stern," as though the creed of Christ's people maintained both its traditional refusal to violate the Second Commandment, and its traditional affirmation of its not-to-be-named God. With the *Judea*, Conrad sinks the romance of youth's illusions, but like all losses in Conrad this submersion in the destructive element is curiously dialectical, since only experiential loss allows for the compensation of an imaginative gain in the representation of artistic truth. Originally the ephebe of Flaubert and of Flaubert's "son," Maupassant, Conrad was reborn as the narrative disciple of Henry James, the James of *The Spoils of Poynton* and *What Maisie Knew*, rather than the James of the final phase.

Ian Watt convincingly traces the genesis of Marlow to the way that "James developed the indirect narrative approach through the sensitive central intelligence of one of the characters." Marlow, whom James derided as "that preposterous magic mariner," actually represents Conrad's swerve away from the excessive strength of James's influence upon him. By always "mixing himself up with the narrative," in James's words, Marlow guarantees an enigmatic reserve that increases the distance between the impressionistic techniques of Conrad and James. Though there is little valid comparison that can be made between Conrad's greatest achievements and the hesitant, barely fictional status of Pater's *Marius the Epicurean*, Conrad's impressionism is as extreme and solipsistic as Pater's. There is a definite parallel between the fates of Sebastian Van Storck (in Pater's *Imaginary Portraits*) and Decoud in *Nostromo*.

In his 1897 "Preface" to *The Nigger of the "Narcissus,"* Conrad famously insisted that his creative task was "before all to make you see." He presumably was aware that he thus joined himself to a line of prose seers whose latest representatives were Carlyle, Ruskin, and Pater. There is a movement in that group from Carlyle's exuberant "Natural Supernaturalism" through Ruskin's paganization of Evangelical fervor to Pater's evasive and skeptical Epicurean materialism, with its eloquent suggestion that all we can see is the flux of sensations. Conrad exceeds Pater in the reduction of impressionism to a state of consciousness where the seeing narrator is hopelessly mixed up with the seen narrative. James may seem an impressionist when compared to Flaubert, but alongside of Conrad he is clearly shown to be a kind of Platonist, imposing forms and resolutions upon the flux of human relations by an exquisite formal geometry altogether his own.

To observe that Conrad is metaphysically less of an idealist is hardly to argue that he is necessarily a stronger novelist than his master, James. It may suggest though that Conrad's originality is more disturbing than that of James, and may help explain why Conrad, rather than James, became the dominant influence upon the generation of American novelists that included Hemingway, Fitzgerald, and Faulkner. The cosmos of *The Sun Also Rises*, *The Great Gatsby*, and *As I Lay Dying* derives from *Heart of Darkness* and *Nostromo* rather than from *The Ambassadors* and *The Golden Bowl*. Darl Bundren is the extreme inheritor of Conrad's quest to carry impressionism into its heart of darkness in the human awareness that we are only a flux of sensations gazing outward upon a flux of impressions.

II

Heart of Darkness may always be a critical battleground between readers who regard it as an aesthetic triumph, and those like myself who doubt its ability to rescue us from its own hopeless obscurantism. That Marlow seems, at moments, not to know what he is talking about, is almost certainly one of the narrative's deliberate strengths, but if Conrad also seems finally not to know, then he necessarily loses some of his authority as a storyteller. Perhaps he loses it to death—our death, or our anxiety that he will not sustain the illusion of his fiction's duration long enough for us to sublimate the frustrations it brings us.

These frustrations need not be deprecated. Conrad's diction, normally flawless, is notoriously vague throughout *Heart of Darkness*. E. M. Forster's wicked comment on Conrad's entire work is justified perhaps only when applied to *Heart of Darkness*:

> Misty in the middle as well as at the edges, the secret cask of his genius contains a vapour rather than a jewel. . . . No creed, in fact.

Forster's misty vapor seems to inhabit such Conradian recurrent modifiers as "monstrous," "unspeakable," "atrocious," and many more, but these are minor defects compared to the involuntary self-parody that Conrad inflicts upon himself. There are moments that sound more like James Thurber lovingly satirizing Conrad than like Conrad:

> We had carried Kurtz into the pilot house: there was more air there. Lying on the couch, he stared through the open shutter. There was an eddy in the mass of human bodies, and the woman with helmeted head and tawny cheeks rushed out to the very brink of the stream. She put out her hands, shouted something, and all that wild mob took up the shout in a roaring chorus of articulated, rapid, breathless utterance.
>
> "Do you understand this?" I asked.
>
> He kept on looking out past me with fiery, longing eyes, with a mingled expression of wistfulness and hate. He made no answer, but I saw a smile, a smile of indefinable meaning, appear on his colorless lips that a moment after twitched convulsively. "Do I not?" he said slowly, gasping, as if the words had been torn out of him by a supernatural power.

This cannot be defended as an instance of what Frank Kermode calls a language "needed when Marlow is not equal to the experience described." Has the experience been described here? Smiles of "indefinable meaning" are smiled once too often in a literary text if they are smiled even once. *Heart of Darkness* has taken on some of the power of myth, even if the book is limited by its involuntary obscurantism. It has haunted American literature from T.S. Eliot's poetry through our major novelists of the era 1920 to 1940, on to a line of movies that go from *Citizen Kane* of Orson Welles (a substitute for an abandoned Welles project to film *Heart of Darkness*) on to Coppola's *Apocalypse Now*. In this instance, Conrad's formlessness seems to have worked as an aid, so diffusing his conception as to have made it available to an almost universal audience.

EDWARD W. SAID

Two Visions in Heart of Darkness

Domination and inequities of power and wealth are perennial facts of human society. But in today's global setting they are also interpretable as having something to do with imperialism, its history, its new forms. The nations of contemporary Asia, Latin America, and Africa are politically independent but in many ways are as dominated and dependent as they were when ruled directly by European powers. On the one hand, this is the consequence of self-inflicted wounds, critics like V. S. Naipaul are wont to say: they (everyone knows that "they" means coloreds, wogs, niggers) are to blame for what "they" are, and it's no use droning on about the legacy of imperialism. On the other hand, blaming the Europeans sweepingly for the misfortunes of the present is not much of an alternative. What we need to do is to look at these matters as a network of interdependent histories that it would be inaccurate and senseless to repress, useful and interesting to understand.

The point here is not complicated. If while sitting in Oxford, Paris, or New York you tell Arabs or Africans that they belong to a basically sick or unregenerate culture, you are unlikely to convince them. Even if you prevail over them, they are not going to concede to you your essential superiority or your right to rule them despite your evident wealth and power. The history of this stand-off is manifest throughout colonies where white masters were once unchallenged but finally driven out. Conversely, the triumphant natives

From *Culture and Imperialism*: 19–31. © 1993 by Edward W. Said.

soon enough found that they needed the West and that the idea of total independence was a nationalist fiction designed mainly for what Fanon calls the "nationalist bourgeoisie," who in turn often ran the new countries with a callous, exploitative tyranny reminiscent of the departed masters.

And so in the late twentieth century the imperial cycle of the last century in some way replicates itself, although today there are really no big empty spaces, no expanding frontiers, no exciting new settlements to establish. We live in one global environment with a huge number of ecological, economic, social, and political pressures tearing at its only dimly perceived, basically uninterpreted and uncomprehended fabric. Anyone with even a vague consciousness of this whole is alarmed at how such remorselessly selfish and narrow interests—patriotism, chauvinism, ethnic, religious, and racial hatreds—can in fact lead to mass destructiveness. The world simply cannot afford this many more times.

One should not pretend that models for a harmonious world order are ready at hand, and it would be equally disingenuous to suppose that ideas of peace and community have much of a chance when power is moved to action by aggressive perceptions of "vital national interests" or unlimited sovereignty. The United States' clash with Iraq and Iraq's aggression against Kuwait concerning oil are obvious examples. The wonder of it is that the schooling for such relatively provincial thought and action is still prevalent, unchecked, uncritically accepted, recurringly replicated in the education of generation after generation. We are all taught to venerate our nations and admire our traditions: we are taught to pursue their interests with toughness and in disregard for other societies. A new and in my opinion appalling tribalism is fracturing societies, separating peoples, promoting greed, bloody conflict, and uninteresting assertions of minor ethnic or group particularity. Little time is spent not so much in "learning about other cultures"—the phrase has an inane vagueness to it—but in studying the map of interactions, the actual and often productive traffic occurring on a day-by-day, and even minute-by-minute basis among states, societies, groups, identities.

No one can hold this entire map in his or her head, which is why the geography of empire and the many-sided imperial experience that created its fundamental texture should be considered first in terms of a few salient configurations. Primarily, as we look back at the nineteenth century, we see that the drive toward empire in effect brought most of the earth under the domination of a handful of powers. To get hold of part of what this means, I propose to look at a specific set of rich cultural documents in which the interaction between Europe or America on the one hand and the imperialized world on the other is animated, informed, made explicit as an experience for both sides of the encounter. Yet before I do this, historically and systematically, it is a useful preparation to look at what still remains of imperialism in recent cultural discussion. This is the residuum of a dense, interesting history that is parodoxically global and local at the same time, and it is also a sign of how the imperial past lives on, arousing argument and counter-argument with surprising intensity. Because they are contemporary and easy at hand, these traces of the past in the present point the way to a study of the histories—the plural is used advisedly—created by empire, not just the stories of the white man and woman, but also those of the non-whites whose lands and very being were at issue, even as their claims were denied or ignored.

One significant contemporary debate about the residue of imperialism—the matter of how "natives" are represented in the Western media—illustrates the persistence of such interdependence and overlapping, not only in the debate's content but in its form, not only in what is said but also in how it is said, by whom, where, and for whom. This bears looking into, although it requires a self-discipline not easily come by, so well-developed, tempting, and ready at hand are the confrontational strategies. In 1984, well before *The Satanic Verses* appeared, Salman Rushdie diagnosed the spate of films and articles about the British Raj, including the television series *The Jewel in the Crown* and David Lean's film of *A Passage to India*. Rushdie noted that the nostalgia pressed into service by these affectionate recollections of British rule in India coincided with the Falklands War, and that "the rise of Raj revisionism, exemplified by the huge success of these fictions, is the artistic counterpart to the rise of conservative ideologies in modern Britain." Commentators responded to what they considered Rushdie's wailing and whining in public and seemed to disregard his principal point. Rushdie was trying to make a larger argument, which presumably should have appealed to intellectuals for whom George Orwell's well-known description of the intellectual's place in society as being inside and outside the whale no longer applied; modern reality in Rushdie's terms was actually "whaleless, this world without quiet corners [in which] there can be no easy escapes from history, from hullabaloo, from terrible, unquiet fuss."[27] But Rushdie's main point was not the point considered worth taking up and debating. Instead the main issue for contention was whether things in the Third World hadn't in fact declined after the colonies had been emancipated, and whether it might not be better on the whole to listen to the rare—luckily, I might add, extremely rare—Third World intellectuals who manfully ascribed most of their present barbarities, tyrannies, and degradations to their own native histories, histories that were pretty bad before colonialism and that reverted to that state after colonialism. Hence, ran this argument, better a ruthlessly honest V. S. Naipaul than an absurdly posturing Rushdie.

One could conclude from the emotions stirred up by Rushdie's own case, then and later, that many people in the West came to feel that enough was enough. After Vietnam and Iran—and note here that these labels are usually employed equally to evoke American domestic traumas (the student insurrections of the 1960s, the public anguish about the hostages in the 1970s) as much as international conflict and the "loss" of Vietnam and Iran to radical nationalisms—after Vietnam and Iran, lines had to be defended. Western democracy had taken a beating, and even if the physical damage had been done abroad, there was a sense, as Jimmy Carter once rather oddly put it, of "mutual destruction." This feeling in turn led to Westerners rethinking the whole process of decolonization. Was it not true, ran their new evaluation, that "we" had given "them" progress and modernization? Hadn't we provided them with order and a kind of stability that they haven't been able since to provide for themselves? Wasn't it an atrocious misplaced trust to believe in their capacity for independence, for it had led to Bokassas and Amins, whose intellectual correlates were people like Rushdie? Shouldn't we have held on to the colonies, kept the subject or inferior races in check, remained true to our civilizational responsibilities?

I realize that what I have just reproduced is not entirely the thing itself, but perhaps a caricature. Nevertheless it bears an uncomfortable resemblance to what many people who imagined themselves speaking for the West said. There seemed little skepticism that a monolithic "West" in fact existed, any more than an entire ex-colonial world described in one sweeping generalization after another. The leap to essences and generalizations was accompanied by appeals to an imagined history of Western endowments and free hand-outs, followed by a reprehensible sequence of ungrateful bitings of that grandly giving "Western" hand. "Why don't they appreciate us, after what we did for them?"[28]

How easily so much could be compressed into that simple formula of unappreciated magnanimity! Dismissed or forgotten were the ravaged colonial peoples who for centuries endured summary justice, unending economic oppression, distortion of their social and intimate lives, and a recourseless submission that was the function of unchanging European superiority. Only to keep in mind the millions of Africans who were supplied to the slave trade is to acknowledge the unimaginable cost of maintaining that superiority. Yet dismissed most often are precisely the infinite number of traces in the immensely detailed, violent history of colonial intervention—minute by minute, hour by hour—in the lives of individuals and collectivities, on both sides of the colonial divide.

The thing to be noticed about this kind of contemporary discourse, which assumes the primacy and even the complete centrality of the West, is how totalizing is its form, how all-enveloping its attitudes and gestures, how much it shuts out even as it includes, compresses, and consolidates. We suddenly find ourselves transported backward in time to the late nineteenth century.

This imperial attitude is, I believe, beautifully captured in the complicated and rich narrative form of Conrad's great novella *Heart of Darkness*, written between 1898 and 1899. On the one hand, the narrator Marlow acknowledges the tragic predicament of all speech—that "it is impossible to convey the life-sensation of any given epoch of one's existence—that which makes its truth, its meaning—its subtle and penetrating essence.... We live, as we dream—alone"[29]—yet still manages to convey the enormous power of Kurtz's African experience through his own overmastering narrative of his voyage into the African interior toward Kurtz. This narrative in turn is connected directly with the redemptive force, as well as the waste and horror, of Europe's mission in the dark world. Whatever is lost or elided or even simply made up in Marlow's immensely compelling recitation is compensated for in the narrative's sheer historical momentum, the temporal, forward movement with digressions, descriptions, exciting encounters, and all. Within the narrative of how he journeyed to Kurtz's Inner Station, whose source and authority he now becomes, Marlow moves backward and forward materially in small and large spirals, very much the way episodes in the course of his journey up-river are then incorporated by the principal forward trajectory into what he renders as "the heart of Africa."

Thus Marlow's encounter with the improbably white-suited clerk in the middle of the jungle furnishes him with several digressive paragraphs, as does his meeting later with the semi-crazed, harlequin-like Russian who has been so affected by Kurtz's gifts. Yet underlying Marlow's inconclusiveness, his evasions, his arabesque meditations on his feelings and ideas, is the unrelenting course of the journey itself, which, despite all the many obstacles, is sustained through the jungle, through time, through hardship, to the heart of it all, Kurtz's ivory-trading empire. Conrad wants us to see how Kurtz's great looting adventure, Marlow's journey up the river, and the narrative itself all share a common theme: Europeans performing acts of imperial mastery and will in (or about) Africa.

What makes Conrad different from the other colonial writers who were his contemporaries is that, for reasons having partly to do with the colonialism that turned him, a Polish expatriate, into an employee of the imperial system, he was so self-conscious about what he did. Like most of his other tales, therefore, *Heart of Darkness* cannot just be a straightforward recital of Marlow's adventures: it is also a dramatization of Marlow himself, the former wanderer in colonial regions, telling his story to a group of British listeners at a particular time and in a specific place. That this group of people is drawn largely from the business world is Conrad's way of emphasizing the fact that during the 1890s the business of empire, once an adventurous and often individualistic enterprise, had become the empire of business. (Coincidentally we should note that at about the same time Halford Mackinder, an explorer, geographer, and Liberal Imperialist, gave a series of lectures on imperialism at the London Institute of Bankers:[30] perhaps Conrad knew about this.) Although the almost oppressive force of Marlow's narrative leaves us with a quite accurate sense that there is no way out of the sovereign historical force of imperialism, and that it has the power of a system representing as well as speaking for everything within its dominion, Conrad shows us that what Marlow does is contingent, acted out for a set of like-minded British hearers, and limited to that situation.

Yet neither Conrad nor Marlow gives us a full view of what is outside the world-conquering attitudes embodied by Kurtz, Marlow, the circle of listeners on the deck of the *Nellie*, and Conrad. By that I mean that *Heart of Darkness* works so effectively because its politics and aesthetics are, so to speak, imperialist, which in the closing years of the nineteenth century seemed to be at the same time an aesthetic, politics, and even epistemology, inevitable and unavoidable. For if we cannot truly understand someone else's experience and if we must therefore depend upon the assertive authority of the sort of power that Kurtz wields as a white man in the jungle or that Marlow, another white man, wields as narrator, there is no use looking for other, non-imperialist alternatives; the system has simply eliminated them and made them unthinkable. The circularity, the perfect closure of the whole thing is not only aesthetically but also mentally unassailable.

Conrad is so self-conscious about situating Marlow's tale in a narrative moment that he allows us simultaneously to realize after all that imperialism, far from swallowing up its own history, was taking place in and was circumscribed by a larger history, one just outside the tightly inclusive circle of Europeans on the deck of the *Nellie*. As yet, however, no one seemed to inhabit that region, and so Conrad left it empty.

Conrad could probably never have used Marlow to present anything other than an imperialist world-view, given what was available for either Conrad or Marlow to see of the non-European at the time. Independence was for whites and Europeans; the lesser or subject peoples were to be ruled; science, learning, history emanated from the West. True, Conrad scrupulously recorded the differences between the disgraces of Belgian and British colonial attitudes, but he could only imagine the world carved up into one or another Western sphere of dominion. But because Conrad also had an extraordinarily persistent residual sense of his own exilic marginality, he quite carefully (some would say maddeningly) qualified Marlow's narrative with the provisionality that came from standing at the very juncture of this world with another, unspecified but different. Conrad was certainly not a great imperialist entrepreneur like Cecil Rhodes or Frederick Lugard, even though he understood perfectly how for each of them, in Hannah Arendt's words, to enter "the maelstrom of an unending process of expansion, he will, as it were, cease to be what he was and obey the laws of the process, identify himself with anonymous forces that he is supposed to serve in order to keep the whole process in motion, he will think of himself as mere function, and eventually consider such functionality, such an incarnation of the dynamic trend, his highest possible achievement."[31] Conrad's realization is that if, like narrative, imperialism has monopolized the entire system of representation—which in the case of *Heart of Darkness* allowed it to speak for Africans as well as for Kurtz and the other adventurers, including Marlow and his audience—your self-consciousness as an outsider can allow you actively to comprehend how the machine works, given that you and it are fundamentally not in perfect synchrony or correspondence. Never the wholly incorporated and fully acculturated Englishman, Conrad therefore preserved an ironic distance in each of his works.

The form of Conrad's narrative has thus made it possible to derive two possible arguments, two visions, in the post-colonial world that succeeded his. One argument allows the old imperial enterprise full scope to play itself out conventionally, to render the world as official European or Western imperialism saw it, and to consolidate itself after World War Two. Westerners may have physically left their old colonies in Africa and Asia, but they retained them not only as markets but as locales on the ideological map over which they continued to rule morally and intellectually. "Show me the Zulu Tolstoy," as one American intellectual has recently put it. The assertive sovereign inclusiveness of this argument courses through the words of those who speak today for the West and for what the West did, as well as for what the rest of the world is, was, and may be. The assertions of this discourse exclude what has been represented as "lost" by arguing that the colonial world was in some ways ontologically speaking lost to begin with, irredeemable, irrecusably inferior. Moreover, it focuses not on what was shared in the colonial experience, but on what must never be shared, namely the authority and rectitude that come with greater power and development. Rhetorically, its terms are the organization of political passions, to borrow from Julien Benda's critique of modern intellectuals, terms which, he was sensible enough to know, lead inevitably to mass slaughter, and if not to literal mass slaughter then certainly to rhetorical slaughter.

The second argument is considerably less objectionable. It sees itself as Conrad saw his own narratives, local to a time and place, neither unconditionally true nor unqualifiedly certain. As I have said, Conrad does not give us the sense that he could imagine a fully realized alternative to imperialism: the natives he wrote about in Africa, Asia, or America were incapable of independence, and because he seemed to imagine that European tutelage was a given, he could not foresee what would take place when it came to an end. But come to an end it would, if only because—like all human effort, like speech itself—it would have its moment, then it would have to pass. Since Conrad *dates* imperialism, shows its contingency, records its illusions and tremendous violence and waste (as in *Nostromo*), he permits his later readers to imagine something other than an Africa carved up into dozens of European colonies, even if, for his own part, he had little notion of what that Africa might be.

To return to the first line out of Conrad, the discourse of resurgent empire proves that the nineteenth-century imperial encounter continues today to draw lines and defend barriers. Strangely, it persists also in the enormously complex and quietly interesting interchange between former colonial partners, say between Britain and India, or between France and the Francophone countries of Africa. But these exchanges tend to be overshadowed by the loud antagonisms of the polarized debate of pro- and anti-imperialists, who speak stridently of national destiny, overseas interests, neo-imperialism, and the like, drawing like-minded people—aggressive Westerners and, ironically, those non-Westerners for whom the new nationalist and resurgent Ayatollahs speak—away from the other ongoing interchange. Inside each regrettably constricted camp stand the blameless, the just, the faithful, led by the omnicompetent, those who know the truth about themselves and others; outside stands a miscellaneous bunch of querulous intellectuals and wishy-washy skeptics who go on complaining about the past to little effect.

An important ideological shift occurred during the 1970s and 1980s, accompanying this contraction of horizons in what I have been calling the first of the two lines leading out of *Heart of Darkness*. One can locate it, for instance, in the dramatic change in emphasis and, quite literally, direction among thinkers noted for their radicalism. The later Jean-François Lyotard and Michel Foucault, eminent French philosophers who emerged during the 1960s as apostles of radicalism and intellectual insurgency, describe a striking new lack of faith in what Lyotard calls the great legitimizing narratives of emancipation and enlightenment. Our age, he said in the 1980s, is post-modernist, concerned only with local issues, not with history but with problems to be solved, not with a grand reality but with games.[32] Foucault also turned his attention away from the oppositional forces in modern society which he had studied for their undeterred resistance to exclusion and confinement—delinquents, poets, outcasts, and the like—and decided that since power was everywhere it was probably better to concentrate on the local micro-physics of power that surround the individual. The self was therefore to be studied, cultivated, and, if necessary, refashioned and constituted.[33] In both Lyotard and Foucault we find precisely the same trope employed to explain the disappointment in the politics of liberation: narrative, which posits an enabling beginning point and a vindicating goal, is no longer adequate for plotting the human trajectory in society. There is nothing to look forward to: we are stuck within our circle. And now the line is enclosed by a circle. After years of support for anti-colonial struggles in Algeria, Cuba, Vietnam, Palestine, Iran, which came to represent for many Western intellectuals their deepest engagement in the politics and philosophy of anti-imperialist decolonization, a moment of exhaustion and disappointment was reached.[34] One began to hear and read how futile it was to support revolutions, how barbaric were the new regimes that came to power, how—this is an extreme case—decolonization had benefitted "world communism."

Enter now terrorism and barbarism. Enter also the ex-colonial experts whose well-publicized message was these colonial peoples deserve only colonialism or, since "we" were foolish to pull out of Aden, Algeria, India, Indochina, and everywhere else, it might be a good idea to reinvade their territories. Enter also various experts and theoreticians of the relationship between liberation movements, terrorism, and the KGB. There was a resurgence of sympathy for what Jeane Kirkpatrick called authoritarian (as opposed to totalitarian) regimes who were Western allies. With the onset of Reaganism, Thatcherism, and their correlates, a new phase of history began.

However else it might have been historically understandable, peremptorily withdrawing "the West" from its own experiences in the "peripheral world" certainly was and is not an attractive or edifying activity for an intellectual today. It shuts out the possibility of knowledge and of discovery of what it means to be outside the whale. Let us return to Rushdie for another insight:

> We see that it can be as false to create a politics-free fictional universe as to create one in which nobody needs to work or eat or hate or love or sleep. Outside the whale it becomes necessary, and even exhilarating, to grapple with the special problems created by the incorporation of political material, because politics is by turns farce and tragedy, and sometimes (e.g., Zia's Pakistan) both at once. Outside the whale the writer is obliged to accept that he (or she) is part of the crowd, part of the ocean, part of the storm, so that objectivity becomes a great dream, like perfection, an unattainable goal for which one must struggle in spite of the impossibility of success. Outside the whale is the world of Samuel Beckett's famous formula: *I can't go on, I'll go on.*[35]

The terms of Rushdie's description, while they borrow from Orwell, seem to me to resonate even more interestingly with Conrad. For here is the second consequence, the second line leading out of Conrad's narrative form; in its explicit references to the outside, it points to a perspective outside the basically imperialist representations provided by Marlow and his listeners. It is a profoundly secular perspective, and it is beholden neither to notions about historical destiny and the essentialism that destiny always seems to entail, nor to historical indifference and resignation. Being on the inside shuts out the full experience of imperialism, edits it and subordinates it to the dominance of one Eurocentric and totalizing view; this other perspective suggests the presence of a field without special historical privileges for one party.

I don't want to overinterpret Rushdie, or put ideas in his prose that he may not have intended. In this controversy with the local British media (before *The Satanic Verses* sent him into hiding), he claimed that he could not recognize the truth of his own experience in the popular media representations of India. Now I myself would go further and say that it is one of the virtues of such conjunctures of politics with culture and aesthetics that they permit the disclosure of a common ground obscured by the controversy itself. Perhaps it is especially hard for the combatants directly involved to see this common ground when they are fighting back more than reflecting. I can perfectly understand the anger that fuelled Rushdie's argument because like him I feel outnumbered and out-organized by a prevailing Western consensus that has come to regard the Third World as an atrocious nuisance, a culturally and politically inferior place. Whereas we write and speak as members of a small minority of marginal voices, our journalistic and academic critics belong to a wealthy system of interlocking informational and academic resources with newspapers, television networks, journals of opinion, and institutes at its disposal. Most of them have now taken up a strident chorus of rightward-tending damnation, in which they separate what is non-white, non-Western, and non-Judeo-Christian from the acceptable and designated Western ethos, then herd it all together under various demeaning rubrics such as terrorist, marginal, second-rate, or unimportant. To attack what is contained in these categories is to defend the Western spirit.

Let us return to Conrad and to what I have been referring to as the second, less imperialistically assertive possibility offered by *Heart of Darkness*. Recall once again that Conrad sets the story on the deck of a boat anchored in the Thames; as Marlow tells his story the sun sets, and by the end of the narrative the heart of darkness has reappeared in England; outside the group of Marlow's listeners lies an undefined and unclear world. Conrad sometimes seems to want to fold that world into the imperial metropolitan discourse represented by Marlow, but by virtue of his own dislocated subjectivity he resists the effort and succeeds in so doing, I have always believed, largely through formal devices. Conrad's self-consciously circular narrative forms draw attention to themselves as artificial constructions, encouraging us to sense the potential of a reality that seemed inaccessible to imperialism, just beyond its control, and that only well after Conrad's death in 1924 acquired a substantial presence.

This needs more explanation. Despite their European names and mannerisms, Conrad's narrators are not average unreflecting witnesses of European imperialism. They do not simply accept what goes on in the name of the imperial idea: they think about it a lot, they worry about it, they are actually quite anxious about whether they can make it seem like a routine thing. But it never is. Conrad's way of demonstrating this discrepancy between the orthodox and his own views of empire is to keep drawing attention to how ideas and values are constructed (and deconstructed) through dislocations in the narrator's language. In addition, the recitations are meticulously staged: the narrator is a speaker whose audience and the reason for their being together, the quality of whose voice, the effect of what he says—are all important and even insistent aspects of the story he tells. Marlow, for example, is never straightforward. He alternates between garrulity and stunning eloquence, and rarely resists making peculiar things seem more peculiar by surprisingly misstating them, or rendering them vague and contradictory. Thus, he says, a French warship fires "into a continent"; Kurtz's eloquence is enlightening as well as fraudulent; and so on—his speech so full of these odd discrepancies (well discussed by Ian Watt as "delayed decoding"[36]) that the net effect is to leave his immediate audience as well as the reader with the acute sense that what he is presenting is not quite as it should be or appears to be.

Yet the whole point of what Kurtz and Marlow talk about is in fact imperial mastery, white European *over* black Africans, and their ivory, civilization *over* the primitive dark continent. By accentuating the discrepancy between the official "idea" of empire and the remarkably disorienting actuality of Africa, Marlow unsettles the reader's sense not only of the very idea of empire, but of something more basic, reality itself. For if Conrad can show that all human activity depends on controlling a radically unstable reality to which words approximate only by will or convention, the same is true of empire, of venerating the idea, and so forth. With Conrad, then, we are in a world being made and unmade more or less all the time. What appears stable and secure—the policeman at the corner, for instance—is only slightly more secure than the white men in the jungle, and requires the same continuous (but precarious) triumph over an all-pervading darkness, which by the end of the tale is shown to be the same in London and in Africa.

Conrad's genius allowed him to realize that the ever-present darkness could be colonized or illuminated—*Heart of Darkness* is full of references to the *mission civilisatrice*, to benevolent as well as cruel schemes to bring light to the dark places and peoples of this world by acts of will and deployments of power—but that it also had to be acknowledged as independent. Kurtz and Marlow acknowledge the darkness, the former as he is dying, the latter as he reflects retrospectively on the meaning of Kurtz's final words. They (and of course Conrad) are ahead of their time in understanding that what they call "the darkness" has an autonomy of its own, and can reinvade and reclaim what imperialism had taken for *its* own. But Marlow and Kurtz are also creatures of their time and cannot take the next step, which would be to recognize that what they saw, disablingly and disparagingly, as a non-European "darkness" was in fact a non-European world *resisting* imperialism so as one day to regain sovereignty and independence, and not, as Conrad reductively says, to reestablish the darkness. Conrad's tragic limitation is that even though he could see clearly that on one level imperialism was essentially pure dominance and land-grabbing, he could not then conclude that imperialism had to end so that "natives" could lead lives free from European domination. As a creature of his time, Conrad could not grant the natives their freedom, despite his severe critique of the imperialism that enslaved them.

The cultural and ideological evidence that Conrad was wrong in his Eurocentric way is both impressive and rich. A whole movement, literature, and theory of resistance and response to empire exists—it is the subject of Chapter Three of this book—and in greatly disparate post-colonial regions one sees tremendously energetic efforts to engage with the metropolitan world in equal debate so as to testify to the diversity and differences of the non-European world and to its own agendas, priorities, and history. The purpose of this testimony is to inscribe, reinterpret, and expand the areas of engagement as well as the terrain contested with Europe. Some of this activity—for example, the work of two important and active Iranian intellectuals, Ali Shariati and Jalal Ali i-Ahmed, who by means of speeches, books, tapes, and pamphlets prepared the way for the Islamic Revolution—interprets colonialism by asserting the absolute opposition of the native culture: the West is an enemy, a disease, an evil. In other instances, novelists like the Kenyan Ngugi and the Sudanese Tayeb Salih appropriate for their fiction such great *topoi* of colonial culture as the quest and the voyage into the unknown, claiming them for their own, post-colonial purposes. Salih's hero in *Season of Migration to the North* does (and is) the reverse of what Kurtz does (and is): the Black man journeys north into white territory.

Between classical nineteenth-century imperialism and what it gave rise to in resistant native cultures, there is thus both a stubborn confrontation and a crossing over in discussion, borrowing back and forth, debate. Many of the most interesting post-colonial writers bear their past within them—as scars of humiliating wounds, as instigation for different practices, as potentially revised visions of the past tending toward a new future, as urgently reinterpretable and redeployable experiences, in which the formerly silent native speaks and acts on territory taken back from the empire. One sees these aspects in Rushdie, Derek Walcott, Aimé Césaire, Chinua Achebe, Pablo Neruda, and Brian Friel. And now these writers can truly read the great colonial masterpieces, which not only misrepresented them but assumed they were unable to read and respond directly to what had been written about them, just as European ethnography presumed the natives' incapacity to intervene in scientific discourse about them. Let us try now to review this new situation more fully.

NOTES

27. Salman Rushdie, "Outside the Whale," in *Imaginary Homelands: Essays and Criticism, 1981–1991* (London: Viking/Granta, 1991), pp. 92, 101.

28. This is the message of Conor Cruise O'Brien's "Why the Wailing Ought to Stop," *The Observer*, June 3, 1984.

29. Joseph Conrad, "Heart of Darkness," in *Youth and Two Other Stories* (Garden City: Doubleday Page, 1925), p. 82.

30. For Mackinder, see Neil Smith, *Uneven Development: Nature, Capital and the Production of Space* (Oxford: Blackwell, 1984), pp. 102–3. Conrad and triumphalist geography are at the heart of Felix Driver, "Geography's Empire: Histories of Geographical Knowledge," *Society and Space*, 1991.

31. Hannah Arendt, *The Origins of Totalitarianism* (1951; new ed. New York: Harcourt Brace Jovanovich, 1973), p. 215. See also Fredric Jameson, *The Political Unconscious: Narrative as a Socially Symbolic Act* (Ithaca: Cornell University Press, 1981), pp. 206–81.

32. Jean-François Lyotard, *The Postmodern Condition: A Report on Knowledge*, trans. Geoff Bennington and Brian Massumi (Minneapolis: University of Minnesota Press, 1984), p. 37.

33. See especially Foucault's late work, *The Care of the Self*, trans. Robert Hurley (New York: Pantheon, 1986). A bold new interpretation arguing that Foucault's entire *oeuvre* is about the self, and his in particular, is advanced in *The Passion of Michel Foucault* by James Miller (New York: Simon & Schuster, 1993).

34. See, for example, Gérard Chaliand, *Revolution in the Third World* (Harmondsworth: Penguin, 1978).

35. Rushdie, "Outside the Whale," pp. 100–101.

36. Ian Watt, *Conrad in the Nineteenth Century* (Berkeley: University of California Press, 1979), pp. 175–79.

CEDRIC WATTS

Heart of Darkness

Conrad's 'Heart of Darkness' is a rich, vivid, layered, paradoxical, and problematic novella or long tale; a mixture of oblique autobiography, traveller's yarn, adventure story, psychological odyssey, political satire, symbolic prose-poem, black comedy, spiritual melodrama, and sceptical meditation. It has proved to be 'ahead of its times': an exceptionally proleptic text. First published in 1899 as a serial in *Blackwood's Edinburgh Magazine*, it became extensively influential during subsequent decades, and reached a zenith of critical acclaim in the period 1950–75. During the final quarter of the twentieth century, however, while its influence became even more pervasive, the tale was vigorously assailed on political grounds by various feminist critics and by some left-wing and Third World commentators.[1] In this essay, I discuss the novella's changing fortunes in 'the whirligig of time' (Feste's phrase from *Twelfth Night*) and argue that even now it retains some capacity to criticize its critics.

I

The phrase 'ahead of its times' first needs defence. What put it *ahead* of them was that it was intelligently *of* them: Conrad addressed issues of the day with such alert adroitness and ambiguity that he anticipated many twentieth-century preoccupations.

From *The Cambridge Companion to Joseph Conrad*, edited by J. H. Stape: 45–62. © 1996 by Cambridge University Press.

In some obvious respects, 'Heart of Darkness' belongs to the late nineteenth century. This is a tale of travel, of adventurous exploration, of an 'outpost of progress'. It draws on the kind of material made popular by Rider Haggard, Rudyard Kipling, R. L. Stevenson, and numerous lesser writers: appropriate fiction for the heyday of imperialism. It is a story of a journey into 'darkest Africa', a region given publicity not only by the explorations of H. M. Stanley but also by the Berlin Conference of 1885, which had recognized the existence of the 'Congo Free State' as the personal possession of King Leopold II of Belgium. It was an era of intense international rivalry for colonial possessions. There was widespread interest in the political, moral, and psychological challenges afforded to Europeans by African colonization. The tale dealt with atavism and decadence, at a time when these topics had been given currency by Zola and the 'Naturalists', by Cesare Lombroso (the criminologist) and Max Nordau (author of *Degeneration*), and by the controversies over the Aesthetic Movement. Nordau, for instance, claimed that civilization was being corrupted by the influence of people who were morally degenerate; and his account of the 'highly-gifted degenerate', the charismatic yet depraved genius, may have influenced Conrad's depiction of Kurtz. A larger matter still was that the popularization of Darwin's theory of evolution had raised widespread anxieties about human nature, its origins, and its future. Finally, the popularization of Lord Kelvin's Second Law of Thermodynamics, the law of entropy, had suggested that eventually, as the sun cooled in the heavens, life would become utterly extinct on this planet, which would be doomed to ultimate darkness. In his tale, Conrad addressed or alluded to all these issues.[2] Characteristically, he had combined popular elements with highly sophisticated analysis. The popular elements included topical allusions, an adventurous narrative, and a range of exotic material. The treatment was challengingly versatile and oblique.

In 'Heart of Darkness', a story is told by a British gentleman to other British gentlemen. The convention of 'the tale within the tale' was familiar and, at that time, particularly appropriate. Among writers of the era whose works Conrad appreciated, it was used by Turgenev, Maupassant, James, Kipling, Crane, Cunninghame Graham, and Wells. This convention was not only a reflection of the social customs of an age of gentlemen's clubs and semi-formal social gatherings at which travellers would meet to compare notes and exchange yarns about foreign experiences. It also emphasized the interplay of personal and social experience, perhaps dramatizing relativism of perception, limitations of knowledge, or conflicts between private and public codes. From its very title onwards ('Heart of Darkness' invokes contradictory notions), the tale is full of paradoxes. And the 1890s were a decade in which paradoxes, whether small or large, abounded in literature. They occurred not merely in the quotable epigrams of Oscar Wilde but in the large-scale paradoxes in the works of, for instance, Samuel Butler, Edward Carpenter, George Bernard Shaw, Thomas Hardy, and Wilde again (in his essay 'The Soul of Man under Socialism', for example). Here ideological contradiction gained rhetorical compression. Previously, Baudelaire had declared that nature provided 'forests of symbols',[3] and, in an era when symbolism in prose and verse commanded fresh interest, Conrad was able to voice his paradoxes not only through explicit statement but also through ambiguous images and many-faceted symbols. The narrative of 'Heart of Darkness' offers, for example, the following paradoxes:

> Civilization can be barbaric. It is both a hypocritical veneer and a valuable achievement to be vigilantly guarded.

> Society saves us from corruption, yet society is corrupt.

> Imperialism may be redeemed by 'an idea at the back of it', but imperialism, irredeemably, is 'robbery with violence'.

> Brotherhood transcends racial differences, but 'we live, as we dream—alone'.

> The truth should be communicated, but women should be denied it. Communication of the essential is impossible.

> Morality is a sham. Without it, human beings become sham humans.

> Awareness is better than unawareness. We may become aware that it is better to be unaware, and we may even learn that ignorance is bliss.

> A person who sells his soul does at least have a soul to sell, and may gain a significance denied to the mediocre.

Repeatedly, images prove paradoxical. The customary associations of white and black, of light and dark, are variously exploited and subverted. The city is 'sepulchral'; London is associated with 'brooding gloom'; and the very title of the tale refers not only to the heart of 'darkest Africa' but also to Kurtz's corruption, to benighted London, and to innumerable kinds of darkness and obscurity, physical, moral, and ontological.

Few prominent features of 'Heart of Darkness' could not be traced back through the nineteenth century into the distant past. Its satiric treatment of imperialism had precedents in Swift's *Gulliver's Travels* (1726), in Voltaire's *Candide* (1759), and in Byron's *Don Juan* (1819–24). The charismatic Kurtz, brilliant yet depraved, corrupted yet fascinating, descends from the 'hero-villains' of Gothic fiction, the most notable of these being Emily Brontë's Heathcliff (who, like Ann Radcliffe's Montoni, is in turn a literary descendant of Milton's Satan, regarded by the Romantics as a sublime rebel). Furthermore, the tale's imagery suggests, Kurtz is a modern Faust, who has sold his soul for power and gratification; so perhaps Charlie Marlow owes a debt to Christopher Marlowe.[4] Even that oblique narrative convention that was so popular in the 1890s can be related to the poetic convention of the dramatic monologue, exploited by Browning and Tennyson, and to the sophisticated employment of multiple narrators in Brontë's *Wuthering Heights*. And the method could be traced via Coleridge's 'Rime of the Ancyent Marinere' back to Chaucer's *Canterbury Tales* and ultimately to the inset narratives of the Homeric epics. Marlow's nightmarish journey is explicitly likened to Dante's imaginary journey in *The Inferno*; and the allusions to ancient Rome help to recall *The Aeneid*, particularly Book VI, in which Aeneas, the legendary imperialist, travels through the underworld.[5]

Of course, the novella also has a diversity of sources in Conrad's personal experience. His scepticism about 'the imperial mission' can be related to the facts that he was born into a Poland which (having been partitioned by Austria, Prussia, and Russia) had vanished from the map of Europe, and that his parents were redoubtable patriots who were exiled by the Russian authorities as punishment for their conspiratorial patriotism. Partly as a result of his parents' political struggle against Russian oppression, both of them died when Conrad was still a boy. Hence his keen sense of the price in human terms exacted by political idealism, and, indeed, by idealism of various kinds. Hence, too, his marked sense of isolation. The contrast between the romanticism of his father, Apollo Korzeniowski, and the astutely sceptical advice of his uncle and guardian, Tadeusz Bobrowski, helped to develop his sense of paradox and ethical conflict.[6] Then Conrad's many years at sea nurtured a respect for the ethical implications of seamanship—for an ethic of work and duty. This is an ethic that Marlow finds sustaining and of which the tale's marine boiler-maker is a modest examplar, and it is made incongruously tangible in that manual of seamanship, by 'Tower, Towson—some such name', found in the heart of the jungle.

'Heart of Darkness' was prompted mainly by Conrad's own journey into the Congo in 1890. During this journey, he noted evidence of atrocities, exploitation, inefficiency, and hypocrisy, and it fully convinced him of the disparity between imperialism's rhetoric and the harsh reality of 'the vilest scramble for loot that ever disfigured the history of human conscience' (*LE*, p. 17).[7] That experience provided a basis for the knowledgeable indignation of

'Heart of Darkness'. Certainly, however, the combination of that indignation and a visionary-symbolic intention results in satiric exaggeration: the inefficiency and incompetence displayed in the tale are so widespread as to make it seem unlikely that the imperialists in Africa could ever establish viable railways, road systems, or towns. Similarly, as Norman Sherry has shown, the real-life counterpart to Kurtz, Georges Antoine Klein, was a counterpart only in the fact that he was an ailing trader in the Congo who had to be transported back downstream on Conrad's vessel and who died on the voyage. There is no evidence at all that he shared Kurtz's brilliance and depravity.[8]

Other, more intimate, personal factors also provided materials for the tale. Conrad was a lively raconteur who used to swap yarns with G. F. W. Hope, W. B. Keen, and C. H. Mears on Hope's yawl, the *Nellie*, anchored in the Thames. Hence, the setting and manner of the tale's opening. Hope was a company director, like the host in the tale; Keen an accountant; Mears a solicitor. Conrad went to Brussels to gain employment with the Belgian company that organized trade in the Congo; Marlow travels to the 'sepulchral city', identifiably Brussels, for his interview. Conrad, like Marlow, gained the interview through the influence exerted by an aunt (though in Conrad's case the person he addressed as 'Aunt'—Marguerite Poradowska—was the wife of a distant cousin). Madame Poradowska was in mourning when Conrad called on her after his journey to the Congo, for her husband had recently died; and, since Conrad was emotionally attracted to her, she evidently provided a model for the bereaved Intended, for whom Marlow feels incipient love.[9] If Marlow has various features in common with Conrad, the depiction of Kurtz was probably inflected by the author's sense of similarity between Kurtz's plight and that of the dedicated creative writer. In a passage of the autobiographical work *A Personal Record* that offers reflections on his own aims as an author, Conrad says:

> In that interior world where his thought and his emotions go seeking for the experience of imagined adventures, there are no policemen, no law, no pressure of circumstance or dread of opinion to keep him within bounds. Who then is going to say Nay to his temptations if not his conscience? (p. xviii)

If, therefore, the tale can be so clearly related to Conrad's own prior experience, to various concerns of the 1890s, and to a diversity of long literary traditions, what makes it proleptic? How did it come to be 'ahead of its times'? The answer lies in the combination of intrinsic and extrinsic factors. The intrinsic factors include: its satiric verve and sceptical boldness; its suggestive density and ambiguity—the layered narrations, ironic meanings, symbolic suggestions; its radical paradoxicality; and its designed opacities. The extrinsic factors include the following. The burgeoning of what became known as cultural Modernism, and the consequent readiness of numerous critics to appreciate and commend the features they recognized as Modernist.[10] The related development of critical procedures that were particularly responsive to ambiguity, irony, and symbolic multiplicity within a work. The increase of scepticism concerning religion, history, civilization, and human nature; though complicated by some religious nostalgia, by surviving modes of faith, and by some humanistic hopes. The general development of antipathy to imperialism: an antipathy that, for many readers, the text seemed to echo (though in course of time other readers disputed this). 'Heart of Darkness' was abundantly suggestive and remarkable quotable. Repeatedly it seemed, prophetically, to sum up areas of experience that gained new prominence in the light of historical events in the twentieth century. If offered a concise iconography of modern corruption and disorder. The tale became an anthology of epitomes.

The First World War showed how men could be engulfed, diminished, and destroyed by man-made organizations and technology. Conrad seemed to have anticipated this in his depiction of the ways in which men in Africa served, and died for, a remorseless organization. He portrays men dwarfed by the system that dominates them and by an alien environment. Hitlerism and the Holocaust seemed to have been anticipated in the depiction of Kurtz's charismatic depravity: Kurtz, potentially 'a splendid leader of an extreme party', celebrated for his intoxicating eloquence, is the persuasive genius whose grandiose ambitions are reduced to the exclamation 'Exterminate all the brutes!'[11] During the century, there was increasing recognition of a vast disparity between the (often religious or idealistic) propaganda of imperialism and its harshly exploitative realities. This too served to vindicate much of the tale, which declared: 'The conquest of the earth . . . mostly means the taking it away from those who have a different complexion or slightly flatter noses than ourselves' (*HD*, p. 140). That 'Heart of Darkness' even seemed to have offered a critical commentary on the Vietnam War was recognized by Francis Ford Coppola's spectacular film, *Apocalypse Now* (1979), which simultaneously generated the film *Hearts of Darkness*, a record of the making of *Apocalypse Now* that was a testament to Kurtzian corruption and decadence in real life. Later, Nicolas Roeg directed another version for the cinema. It seemed that the sombre, sceptical aspects of the tale had been amply vindicated by the follies and brutalities of twentieth-century history.

In 1902, Edward Garnett, Conrad's friend and sometime literary mentor, wrote: '"Heart of Darkness" in the subtlety of its criticism of life is the high-water mark of the author's talent' (Sherry, ed., *Conrad: The Critical Heritage*, p. 133). By 1974, C. B. Cox could confidently declare: 'This masterpiece has become one of those amazing modern fictions, such as Thomas Mann's

Death in Venice or Kafka's *The Trial*, which throw light on the whole nature of twentieth-century art, its problems and achievements' (Introduction, p. vii). Repeatedly, the tale seemed to have heralded twentieth-century cultural preoccupations. Sigmund Freud's emphasis on the divided self, on the striving, lustful, anarchic id seeking gratification despite the countervailing pressure of the ego or super-ego, had been anticipated in the depiction of Kurtz's ferocious fulfilments in the Congo. C. G. Jung, in turn, seemed almost to be recalling Kurtz and the tale's imagery of light and darkness when he emphasized that the 'visionary mode of artistic creation' is

> a strange something that derives its existence from the hinterland of man's mind—that suggests the abyss of time separating us from pre-human ages, or evokes a super-human world of contrasting light and darkness. It is a primordial experience which surpasses man's understanding, and to which he is therefore in danger of succumbing.
>
> (*Modern Man in Search of a Soul*, p. 180)

The interest of Freud and Jung (and later of Northrop Frye, Joseph Campbell, and Claude Lévi-Strauss) in the importance of myth was shared by numerous Modernist writers, and here again Conrad seemed to have anticipated them. In 1923, T. S. Eliot praised James Joyce for developing in *Ulysses* the 'mythic method', whereby references to ancient myths could coordinate works which addressed 'the immense panorama of futility and anarchy which is contemporary history' ('*Ulysses*, order and myth', p. 483). But that readiness to stage ironic contrasts between the mythic past and the materialistic present, a readiness so marked in Eliot's *The Waste Land* itself, was already a feature of 'Heart of Darkness', which, while describing present-day confusion, invoked memories of the Faust myth, *The Divine Comedy*, and *The Aeneid*. Indeed, Eliot acknowledged a debt to Conrad: the original epigraph of *The Waste Land* was a passage from 'Heart of Darkness' that concludes with Kurtz's words, 'The horror! The horror!', and the descriptions of the Thames in 'The Fire Sermon' draw details from the opening of Conrad's tale.[12] More importantly, 'Heart of Darkness' had suggested the appalling paradox that whereas the majority of men who lead secular lives are heading for a death which is extinction, Kurtz has at least the significance granted by the intensity of his evil. If he has sold his soul, at least he had a soul to sell. And this paradox, too, Eliot developed in *The Waste Land* and in his critical essays: 'Damnation itself is an immediate form of salvation—of salvation from the ennui of modern life, because it at last gives some significance to living ... The worst that can be said of most of our malefactors ... is that they are not men enough to be damned' (*Selected Essays*, pp. 427, 429). Graham Greene exploited the same paradox in *Brighton Rock*

(1938), and Greene often acknowledged his debt to Conrad. In the film *The Third Man* (1949), written by Greene and directed by Carol Reed, the villain, Harry Lime, has a Kurtzian charisma, and one of his henchmen is called 'Baron Kurtz'. Lime was played by Orson Welles, who had himself attempted to make a film of 'Heart of Darkness'. In 1899, in its vividly graphic techniques, particularly the rapid montage, the overlapping images, and the symbolic use of colour and *chiaroscuro*, 'Heart of Darkness' had been adventurously cinematic at a time when film—rudimentary then—was not.

Familiar characteristics of Modernist texts are the sense of absurdity or meaninglessness, of human isolation, and of the problematic nature of communication. Eliot, Kafka, Woolf, and Beckett are among the writers who grappled with these matters, all of which had been sharply depicted in 'Heart of Darkness'. The sense of the defilement of the natural environment by man's technology, another powerful feature of the narrative, was later to be addressed by Eliot, Lawrence, Greene, and numerous subsequent writers. Kurtz's words 'The horror! The horror!' were eventually repeated by Colonel Kurtz, played by a mumbling Marlon Brando, in *Apocalypse Now*; but before repeating them, he quoted a few lines from Eliot's poem, 'The Hollow Men'. This made a neat cultural irony, since 'The Hollow Men' takes as its epigraph 'Mistah Kurtz—he dead' and develops the Conradian theme of the absurdity of secular existence.

The tale's cultural echoes extend through time and across continents. Kurtz is a literary father of Thompson, the demoralized imperial idealist in the acclaimed novel of Kenya in the 1950s, *A Grain of Wheat* (1967) by Ngugi wa Thiong'o. Kurtz's report for 'The Society for the Suppression of Savage Customs' has its counterpart in Thompson's essay, 'Prospero in Africa'. Kurtz concludes: 'Exterminate all the brutes!'; Thompson reflects: 'Eliminate the vermin' (pp. 48–50, 117). A radically different novel, Robert Stone's *Dog Soldiers* (1975), a prize-winning thriller depicting drug-driven corruption and brutality in the United States, took as its apt epigraph the following lines from Conrad's tale:

> 'I've seen the devil of violence, and the devil of greed, and the devil of hot desire; but, by all the stars! these were strong, lusty, red-eyed devils, that swayed and drove men—men, I tell you. But as I stood on this hillside, I foresaw that in the blinding sunshine of that land I would become acquainted with a flabby, pretending, weak-eyed devil of a rapacious and pitiless folly.' (p. 155)[13]

II

By the 1970s, 'Heart of Darkness' had accumulated extensive critical acclaim and been widely disseminated as a 'set text' in colleges and universities. It was now 'canonical'. Even if it had flaws (perhaps 'adjectival insistence'),[14] its strengths far exceeded its weaknesses. Its cultural influence was clearly pervasive. This novella served as a reference-point, an anthology of scenes and passages that in various ways epitomized twentieth-century problems and particularly twentieth-century modes of exploitation, corruption, and decadence. Yet, as Feste says in *Twelfth Night*, 'the whirligig of time brings in his revenges', and in the 1970s radical critical attacks on 'Heart of Darkness' developed. For Terry Eagleton, a Marxist, Conrad's art was an art of ideological contradiction resulting in stalemate:

> Conrad neither believes in the cultural superiority of the colonialist nations, nor rejects colonialism outright. The 'message' of *Heart of Darkness* is that Western civilisation is at base as barbarous as African society—a viewpoint which disturbs imperialist assumptions to the precise degree that it reinforces them.
>
> (*Criticism and Ideology*, p. 135)

But already a far more damaging political attack had been made. In a 1975 lecture, the distinguished Nigerian novelist, Chinua Achebe, declared that Conrad was 'a bloody racist' ('An image of Africa', p. 788). Achebe asserted that 'Heart of Darkness' depicts Africa as 'a place of negations ... in comparison with which Europe's own state of spiritual grace will be manifest' (p. 783). The Africans are dehumanized and degraded, seen as grotesques or as a howling mob. They are denied speech, or are granted speech only to condemn themselves out of their own mouths. We see 'Africa as setting and backdrop which eliminates the African as human factor. Africa as a metaphysical battlefield devoid of all recognizable humanity, into which the wandering European enters at his peril' (p. 788). The result, he says, is 'an offensive and totally deplorable book' that promotes racial intolerance and is therefore to be condemned.

Achebe's lecture had a powerful impact, and its text was repeatedly reprinted and widely discussed. 'Heart of Darkness', which had seemed to be bold and astute in its attacks on imperialism, was now revealed as a work that, in the opinion of a leading African writer, was actually pro-imperialist in its endorsement of racial prejudice. The next onslaught came from feminist critics and had a similar basis. While Achebe had seen the Africans as marginalized and demeaningly stereotyped, various feminist critics felt that the tale similarly belittled women. Nina Pelikan Straus, Bette London, Johanna M. Smith, and Elaine Showalter were among those who claimed that 'Heart of Darkness' was not only imperialist but also 'sexist'. Straus declared that male critics had repeatedly become accomplices of Marlow, who 'brings truth to men by virtue of his bringing falsehood to women'

('The exclusion of the Intended', p. 130). Kurtz's Intended, denied a name, is also denied access to truth so as to maintain the dominative brotherhood of males:

> The woman reader ... is in the position to insist that Marlow's cowardice consists of his inability to face the dangerous self that is the form of his own masculinist vulnerability: his own complicity in the racist, sexist, imperialist, and finally libidinally satisfying world he has shared with Kurtz. (p. 135)

Smith, similarly, alleged that the tale 'reveals the collusion of imperialism and patriarchy: Marlow's narrative aims to "colonize" and "pacify" both savage darkness and women' ('Too beautiful altogether', p. 180).

In short, a text that had once appeared to be 'ahead of its times', a nineteenth-century tale that anticipated twentieth-century cultural developments and epitomized twentieth-century concerns, now seemed to be dated—outstripped by recent advances. A text that had so often been praised for its political radicalism now looked politically reactionary. The problems raised by the controversy over the merits of 'Heart of Darkness' were now problems not merely about the reading of details but also about the very basis of evaluation of literary texts, about the relationship between literary appreciation and moral/political judgement.

III

If we re-read 'Heart of Darkness' in the light of Achebe's comments, various disturbing features soon gain prominence. For example, although the Europeans manifest various kinds of corruption and turpitude, the Faustian theme associates supernatural evil with the African wilderness. The dying Kurtz crawls ashore towards some ritual ceremony, and Marlow tries to head him off:

> 'I tried to break the spell—the heavy, mute spell of the wilderness—that seemed to draw him to its pitiless breast by the awakening of forgotten and brutal instincts, by the memory of gratified and monstrous passions. This alone, I was convinced, had driven him out to the edge of the forest, to the bush, towards the gleam of fires, the throb of drums, the drone of weird incantations; this alone had beguiled his unlawful soul beyond the bounds of permitted aspirations'. (p. 234)

And within the wilderness:

'A black figure stood up, strode on long black legs, waving long black arms, across the glow. It had horns—antelope horns, I think—on its head. Some sorcerer, some witch-man, no doubt: it looked fiend-like enough'. (p. 233)

In religious matters, Marlow seems usually a sceptic. Certainly there is an atheistic implication in his remark that life is 'that mysterious arrangement of merciless logic for a futile purpose'. Yet, where Kurtz's depravity is concerned, Marlow seems willing to endorse a belief in supernatural evil—and that evil is specifically associated with the people of the African jungle. A sceptical reader today might conclude that we are being offered not only a mystification of corruption, but also a racist mystification. One problem here, however, is that the observations quoted are Marlow's, and they thus lack the authority that would be granted by an 'omniscient narrator'. Achebe says that Conrad 'neglects to hint however subtly or tentatively at an alternative frame of reference ... Marlow seems to me to enjoy Conrad's complete confidence' (p. 787). Against this, however, one might object that Conrad has deliberately opted for doubly oblique narration. Marlow's tale, which is interrupted by dissenting comments by his hearers, is being reported to us by an anonymous character. Marlow himself has explicitly drawn attention to the difficulty of seeing truly and reporting correctly, and he is known for his 'inconclusive' narratives. His tone when describing Kurtz's last hours is more insistently rhetorical and less observantly acute than at other times. The general effect of the oblique procedures may be to make us think: 'Marlow can probably be trusted most of the time, but we need to keep up our guard. He isn't fully reliable'. Indeed, Conrad took greater pains than did most users of the oblique narrative convention to preserve the possibility of critical distance between the reader and the fictional narrator.

Nevertheless, Achebe forcefully exposed the text's temporality. A number of features, including Marlow's casual use of the term 'nigger', clearly reveal the tale's Victorian provenance. Its defenders now ran the risk of using a suspect logic. When Marlow said things of which they approved, they might give Conrad credit; when he said things that embarrassed them, they might cite the oblique convention, blame Marlow, and exonerate Conrad. Clearly, such logic could be neatly reversed by their opponents.

Achebe's telling attack was fierce and sweeping, and deliberately polemical, and he later moderated its ferocity.[15] Other Third World writers, including Ngugi wa Thiong'o, Wilson Harris, Frances B. Singh, and C. P. Sarvan, argued that while Conrad was certainly ambivalent on racial matters, 'Heart of Darkness' was progressive in its satiric accounts of the colonialists. Singh noted that though 'Heart of Darkness' was vulnerable in several respects, including the association of Africans with supernatural evil, the story should remain in 'the canon of works indicting colonialism'. Sarvan concluded: 'Conrad was not entirely immune to the infection of the beliefs and attitudes of his age, but he was ahead of most in trying to break free'.[16] To be fair to 'Heart of Darkness', as to any literary text, we need to take account of its date. As Sarvan indicates, relative to the standards prevailing in the 1890s, the heyday of Victorian imperialism, 'Heart of Darkness' was indeed progressive in its criticism of imperialist activities in Africa, and, implicitly, of imperialist activities generally. Conrad was writing at a time when most British people, including many socialists, would have regarded imperialism as an admirable enterprise. He was also helping the cause of Africans in the Congo by drawing attention to their ill-treatment. In practice, the tale contributed to the international protest campaign that strove to curb Belgian excesses there. E. D. Morel, leader of the Congo Reform Association, stated that 'Heart of Darkness' was 'the most powerful thing ever written on the subject'. Conrad sent encouraging letters to his acquaintance (and Morel's collaborator in the campaign), Roger Casement, who in 1904 published a parliamentary report documenting atrocities committed by Belgian administrators.[17] Achebe says that 'Heart of Darkness' marginalizes the Africans, but Marlow gives them prominence when he describes, with telling vividness, the plight of the chain-gang and of the exploited workers dying in the grove. What the other Europeans choose to ignore, Marlow observes with sardonic indignation. Relegation, which is criticized, is a theme of the narrative.

That the tale appeared in 1899 offers some defence against feminists' attacks, too, though it is defence and not vindication. Marlow's patronizing views of women, which might well have been quite widely shared by men of that time, are problematized by the text in ways that yield ironies that feminist critics could exploit. Marlow, who says that women are 'out of touch with truth ... in a world of their own' (p. 148), depends on his aunt for a job, and therefore her world is also his. Furthermore, Marlow's lie to the Intended—the cause of so much critical debate—is presented in a debate-provoking way. Marlow registers confusion ('It seemed ... that the heavens would fall'; 'The heavens do not fall for such a trifle'), and he had previously said 'I hate, detest, and can't bear a lie', so his own words expose a double standard by which women are (a) culpably ignorant of truth, and (b) in need of falsehood supplied by males. In any case, characteristically 'virile' activities of men—colonial warfare and the conquest of the 'wilderness'—have been depicted by Marlow as virtually deranged in their destructive futility.

A larger question is raised by these political criticisms of 'Heart of Darkness'. A standard procedure, illustrated by Achebe and Straus, is to judge the tale according to whether its inferred political outlook tallies with that of the critic: to the extent that the critic's views are reflected, the tale is commended; to the extent that they are not, the tale is condemned. This procedure is familiar but odd. It assumes the general validity of the critic's outlook; but different people have different outlooks. Moreover, the critic's outlook may not remain constant, but may be modified by experience, including encounters with literary works. In this respect, 'Heart of Darkness' seems to ambush its adversaries. Marlow has been changed by his experience of Africa, and is still being changed. One of the subtlest features of the text is the dramatization of his uncertainties, of his tentativeness, of his groping for affirmations that his own narrative subsequently questions. Through Marlow, this liminal and protean novella renders the process of teaching and learning, and of negotiating alternative viewpoints. To take an obvious example: he offers conflicting interpretations of Kurtz's cry, 'The horror! The horror!' Perhaps they refer to Kurtz's corruption, perhaps to the horror of a senseless universe. But there may be another meaning: no final resolution is offered. Marlow addresses a group of friends on a vessel. They may not share his views; and, indeed, they voice dissent—'Try to be civil'; 'Absurd'. A commentator who declares Conrad 'racist' or 'sexist' may be imposing on Conrad readily available stereotypes, but, at its best, the tale questions the process of imposing stereotypes. Such phrases as 'weaning those ignorant millions', 'enemies, criminals, workers . . . rebels', 'unsound method' or 'leader of an extreme party' are invested with sardonic irony. In addition, a political commentator on the text may seem imperialistic in seeking to incorporate literary terrain within the territory of his or her own personal value-system. If we abolished all those past texts that, to our fallible understandings, failed to endorse present values or prejudices, few works would survive. A literary work may have a diversity of political implications and consequences, but it is not a political manifesto. It is an imaginative work that offers a voluntary and hypothetical experience. Its linguistic texture may be progressive when its readily paraphrasable content may not. All its implications remain within the invisible quotation marks of the fictional. In other works, the same author could, of course, deploy quite different materials with contrasting implications. In 'Heart of Darkness', Marlow says that women are out of touch with truth; but in *Chance*, he says that women see 'the whole truth', whereas men live in a 'fool's paradise' (p. 144). Meanwhile, in 1910, Conrad signed a formal letter to the Prime Minister, Herbert Asquith, advocating votes for women (*Letters*, IV, p. 327).[18] Awareness of Conrad's complexity may entail recognition of a currently widespread critical habit: the reductive falsification of the past in an attempt to vindicate the political gestures of the present. 'Heart of Darkness' reminds us that this habit resembles an earlier one: the adoption of a demeaning attitude to colonized people in the attempt to vindicate the exploitative actions of the colonizer. The 'pilgrims' in the tale have fathered some of the pundits of today.

We read fiction for pleasures of diverse kinds; and Conrad earned his living as an entertainer, not as a writer of religious or political tracts. The pleasures generated by 'Heart of Darkness' have many sources. They lie in part in its evocative vividness, its modes of suspense, its originality, and its power to provoke thought. Paraphrase is a necessary critical tool, but paraphrase is never an equivalent of the original, whose vitality lies in its combination of particular and general, of rational and emotional. A political scansion of the work is not the only mode of scansion, nor is it necessarily the most illuminating. Literary criticism has an identity distinct from political advocacy, just as creative writing is distinct from political non-fiction. As the text moves through time, the changing historical and cultural circumstances will variously increase and reduce its cogency. Texts may thus apparently die for a period and then regain their vitality. Shakespeare's *King Lear* vanished from the stage for about 150 years, and audiences seeing *King Lear* in the eighteenth century saw Nahum Tate's play, not Shakespeare's. May Sinclair's fine novel, *Life and Death of Harriett Frean* (1922), was neglected for decades until Virago Press republished it. The reputation of 'Heart of Darkness' is now a matter of controversy, and its standing may decline; but its complexity guarantees that it will prove fruitful to many readers for a long time yet.

As we have seen, the very ambiguity of that title, 'Heart of Darkness' (originally 'The Heart of Darkness'), heralded that complexity. The titular phrase then evoked the interior of 'darkest Africa'; but it also portended the corruption of Kurtz, and the tale begins with visual reminders of ways in which London, centre of the empire 'on which the sun never sets', can itself be a heart of darkness—palled in 'brooding gloom'. So, from the outset, the narrative probes, questions, and subverts familiar contrasts between the far and the near, between the 'savage' and the 'civilized', between the tropical and the urban. Repeatedly, the tale's descriptions gain vividness by Conrad's use of delayed decoding, a technique whereby effect precedes cause.[19] He presents first the impact of an event, and only after a delay does he offer its explanation. This is exemplified by the descriptions of, for example, the chaos at the Outer Station, eventually explained as railway-building, or of the exploited Africans in the chain-gang, who 'were called criminals'. The technique lends graphic vividness and psychological realism to the process of perception, but it also emphasizes an ironic disparity, or possible disparity, between the events that occur and their conventional interpretation. Delayed decoding is used in numerous ways: in the treatment of small details, of large events, and even of plot sequences within the tale. Sometimes the irony lies in the fact that the interpretation is tardy, or inadequate, or constitutes a reductive falsification. And here lies a warning for commentators on 'Heart of Darkness'. One of the features that made it outstanding among texts of the 1890s was its recognition of the disparities between the realities of experience and the inadequacies of conventional interpretations of it. The tale repeatedly implies an irreducible excess that eludes summary. It may thus warn commentators that they, confined to the limited discourse of rational non-fictional prose, are likely to be outdistanced by the multiple resources of the fictional text. The anonymous narrator speaks with romantic eloquence of all the great men who have sailed forth on the Thames, but Marlow interjects 'And this also . . . has been one of the dark places of the earth', and proceeds to remind him that Britain would once have seemed as savage a wilderness to Roman colonizers as Africa now seems to Europeans. This is a rebuke to empire-builders and to believers in the durability of civilization; it invokes a humiliating chronological perspective; and it may jolt the reader into circumspection.

Reflections on this passage might induce caution in any commentator who initially fails to relate 'Heart of Darkness' fairly to the time of its writing, or who assumes the superiority of a present-day viewpoint that is itself a product of the times: 'We live in the flicker'. As 'Heart of Darkness' repeatedly implies, a value judgement cannot, in logic, be deduced from a statement of fact. The narrative is partly about the struggle to maintain a humane morality when that morality no longer seems to bear guaranteed validity. In this respect, 'Heart of Darkness' remains cogent and may teach circumspection to its critics. The tale has sombre implications, and so has the story of its reception over the years, but the eloquence, virtuosity, and intensity with which 'Heart of Darkness' addressed its era were exemplary, and seem likely to ensure its longevity.

NOTES

1. This novella's critical fortunes may be traced in Sherry, ed., *Conrad: The Critical Heritage*, Harkness, ed., *Conrad's 'Heart of Darkness' and the Critics*, Murfin, ed., *Joseph Conrad: 'Heart of Darkness': A Case Study in Contemporary Criticism*, Bloom, ed., *Joseph Conrad's 'Heart of Darkness'*, Carabine, ed., *Joseph Conrad: Critical Assessments*, Kimbrough's Norton volumes of 1963, 1971, and 1988, and Burden, *'Heart of Darkness': An Introduction to the Variety of Criticism*. Fothergill's *Heart of Darkness* provides a useful introductory summary.

2. Documents concerning the history of the 'Congo Free State' and Conrad's journey in that region are reprinted in *Heart of Darkness*, Kimbrough, ed., *Joseph Conrad's 'Heart of Darkness'*, pp. 78–192. For the cultural background, see Watt, *Conrad in the Nineteenth Century*. On Nordau and Kelvin, see Watts, *Conrad's 'Heart of Darkness': A Critical and Contextual Discussion*, pp. 132–4, 14–15. (Nordau had written to Conrad to congratulate him on *The Nigger of the 'Narcissus'*.)

3. Baudelaire, 'Correspondances', *Les Fleurs du mal*, pp. 17–18.

4. See Watts, *The Deceptive Text*, pp. 74–82.

5. See Evans, 'Conrad's underworld', and Feder, 'Marlow's descent into hell'.

6. On the Polish background, see Najder, *Joseph Conrad: A Chronicle*, pp. 2–53 *et passim*.

7. See 'The Congo Diary' in Kimbrough, ed., *Joseph Conrad's 'Heart of Darkness'*, pp. 159–66.

8. Ch. 1–12 of Sherry's *Conrad's Western World* deal with the fictional transformation of factual materials concerning Africa. Klein is discussed on pp. 72–8.

9. Conrad said that there was 'a mere shadow of love interest just in the last pages' (*Letters*, II, pp. 145–6).

10. On Conrad's relation to Modernism, see Graham, ch. 11 of this volume, and Watt, *Conrad in the Nineteenth Century*, pp. 32–3 *et passim*.

11. This link was recognized in George Steiner's novel, *The Portage to San Cristobal of A. H.* (1981), in which the Kurtzian role is taken by an aged but still eloquent Adolf Hitler, discovered in the depths of the jungle.

12. See Eliot, *The Waste Land*, pp. 3, 125.

13. The version in Stone (p. vii) has minor misquotations.

14. 'So we have an adjectival and worse than supererogatory insistence on "unspeakable rites", "unspeakable secrets", "monstrous passions", "inconceivable mystery", and so on . . . Conrad . . . is intent on making a virtue out of not knowing what he means', Leavis, *The Great Tradition*, pp. 198–9.

15. For example, the revised version in Kimbrough, ed., *Joseph Conrad's 'Heart of Darkness'*, pp. 251–62, deletes a passage linking Conrad to 'men in Nazi Germany who lent their talent to the service of virulent racism', and concedes that 'Heart of Darkness' has 'memorably good passages and moments'. The phrase 'a bloody racist' became 'a thoroughgoing racist'. Carabine, ed., *Joseph Conrad: Critical Assessments*, II, also prints the revised version although erroneously identifying it as the 1977 text.

16. Sarvan in Kimbrough, ed., *Joseph Conrad's 'Heart of Darkness'*, p. 285. Ngugi wa Thiong'o is cited on p. 285; articles by Harris and Singh are reprinted, pp. 262–80. Carabine, ed., *Joseph Conrad: Critical Assessments*, II, pp. 405–80, also offers a range of responses to Achebe.

17. On Morel, see Hawkins, 'Conrad's critique of imperialism', p. 293. On Casement, see *Letters*, III, pp. 87, 95–7, 101–3.

18. See also Davies, 'Conrad, *Chance*, and women readers'.

19. On delayed decoding, see Watt, *Conrad in the Nineteenth Century*, pp. 175–9, 270–1, 357, and Watts, *The Deceptive Text*, pp. 43–6, and *A Preface to Conrad*, pp. 114–17.

Works Cited

Achebe, Chinua. 'An image of Africa: racism in Conrad's "Heart of Darkness"'. *Massachusetts Review* 17.4 (1977), 782–94. Reprinted (revised) in Kimbrough, ed., *Joseph Conrad's 'Heart of Darkness'*, pp. 251–62.

Baudelaire, Charles. *Les Fleurs du mal.* 1857. Paris: Aux quais de Paris, 1957.

Bloom, Harold, ed. *Joseph Conrad's 'Heart of Darkness'.* New York: Chelsea House, 1987.

Burden, Robert. *'Heart of Darkness': An Introduction to the Variety of Criticism.* London: Macmillan, 1991.

Carabine, Keith, ed. *Joseph Conrad: Critical Assessments.* 4 vols. Robertsbridge: Helm Information, 1992.

Conrad, Joseph. *Chance.* 1914. Ed. Martin Ray. Oxford: Oxford University Press, 1988.

———. *'Heart of Darkness' and Other Tales.* Ed. Cedric Watts. Oxford: Oxford University Press, 1990.

———. 'A Familiar Preface'. *'The Mirror of the Sea' and 'A Personal Record'.* 1906 and 1912. Ed. Zdzislaw Najder. Oxford: Oxford University Press, 1988, pp. xi–xxi.

———. 'Geography and some explorers'. 1924. *Last Essays*. Ed. Richard Curle. London: Dent, 1926. Reprinted 1955, pp. 1–22.

Cox, C. B. Introduction. *Youth: A Narrative/Heart of Darkness/The End of the Tether*. London: Dent; Vermont: Tuttle, 1974.

Davies, Laurence. 'Conrad, *Chance*, and women readers'. *The Conradian* 17.1 (1993), 75–88.

Eagleton, Terry. *Criticism and Ideology: A Study in Marxist Literary Theory*. London: Verso, 1976.

Eliot, T. S. *The Waste Land: A Facsimile and Transcript of the Original Drafts including the Annotations of Ezra Pound*. Ed. Valerie Eliot. London: Faber & Faber, 1971.

———. *Selected Essays*. London: Faber & Faber, 1951.

———. '*Ulysses*, order and myth'. *The Dial* 75 (1923), 480–3.

Evans, Robert O. 'Conrad's underworld'. *Modern Fiction Studies* 2.2 (1956), 56–92.

Feder, Lillian. 'Marlow's descent into hell'. *Nineteenth Century Fiction* 9.4 (1955), 280–92.

Fothergill, Anthony. *Heart of Darkness*. Milton Keynes: Open University Press, 1989.

Harkness, Bruce, ed. *Conrad's 'Heart of Darkness' and the Critics*. Belmont, CA: Wadsworth, 1960.

Harris, Wilson. 'The frontier on which "Heart of Darkness" stands'. *Research on African Literatures* 12 (1981), 86–92. Reprinted Kimbrough, ed., *Joseph Conrad's 'Heart of Darkness'*, pp. 262–8.

Hawkins, Hunt. 'Conrad's critique of imperialism'. *PMLA* 94 (1979), 286–99.

Jung, C. B. *Modern Man in Search of a Soul*. London: Routledge & Kegan Paul, 1933. Reprinted 1966.

Kimbrough, Robert, ed. *Joseph Conrad's 'Heart of Darkness'*. 3rd edn. New York: Norton, 1988.

Leavis, F. R. *The Great Tradition: George Eliot, Henry James, Joseph Conrad*. London: Chatto & Windus; New York: G. W. Stewart, 1948. Reprinted Harmondsworth: Penguin Books, 1962.

London, Bette. *The Appropriated Voice: Narrative Authority in Conrad, Forster, and Woolf*. Ann Arbor: University of Michigan Press, 1990.

Murfin, Ross C., ed. *Joseph Conrad: 'Heart of Darkness': A Case Study in Contemporary Criticism*. New York: Bedford Books of St Martin's Press, 1989.

Najder, Zdzislaw. *Joseph Conrad: A Chronicle*. Tr. Halina Carroll-Najder. New Brunswick, NJ: Rutgers University Press; Cambridge: Cambridge University Press, 1983.

Sarvan, C. P. 'Racism and the *Heart of Darkness*'. *International Fiction Review* 7 (1980), 6–10. Reprinted Kimbrough, ed., *Joseph Conrad's 'Heart of Darkness'*, pp. 280–5.

Sherry, Norman. *Conrad's Western World*. Cambridge: Cambridge University Press, 1971.

———, ed. *Conrad: The Critical Heritage*. London: Routledge & Kegan Paul, 1973.

Showalter, Elaine. *Sexual Anarchy*. London: Bloomsbury, 1991.

Smith, Johanna M. '"Too beautiful altogether": patriarchal ideology in "Heart of Darkness."' In *Joseph Conrad: 'Heart of Darkness': A Case Study in Contemporary Criticism*. Ed. Ross C. Murfin. New York: Bedford Books of St Martin's Press, 1989, pp. 179–95.

Steiner, George. *The Portage to San Cristobal of A. H.* London: Faber & Faber, 1981.

Stone, Robert. *Dog Soldiers*. London: Secker & Warburg, 1975. Reprinted London: Pan Books, 1988.

Straus, Nina Pelikan. 'The exclusion of the Intended from secret sharing in Conrad's "Heart of Darkness"'. *Novel* 20.2 (1987), 123–37.

Thiong'o, Ngugi wa. *A Grain of Wheat*. London: Heinemann, 1967. Reset 1975.

Watt, Ian. *Conrad in the Nineteenth Century*. Berkeley: University of California Press, 1979; London: Chatto & Windus, 1980.

Watts, Cedric. *Conrad's 'Heart of Darkness': A Critical and Contextual Discussion*. Milan: Mursia, 1977.

———. *The Deceptive Text: An Introduction to Covert Plots*. Brighton: Harvester; Totowa, NJ: Barnes & Noble, 1984.

———. *A Preface to Conrad*. 2nd edn. London: Longman, 1993.

JOHN G. PETERS

The Opaque and the Clear:
The White Fog Incident in
Conrad's "Heart of Darkness"

And nothing is but what is not.

—Shakespeare, Macbeth 1:3

For a short space in part two of "Heart of Darkness," Marlow relates an event that occurred on his journey up the Congo River (101–07). One morning, the men on the steamer find themselves caught in a thick, white fog. Ian Watt remarks, "Mist or haze is a very persistent image in Conrad" (Watt 169).[1] These mists, hazes, and fogs serve several purposes. Of the fog that appears near the end of "An Outpost of Progress," Edward Said suggests, "After Carlier's accidental murder, Kayerts' confusion is given concrete embodiment in a thick fog that descends, perhaps intended to represent the sinister shadow of truth he cannot tolerate" (Said 143). Said believes that the fog in this scene obscures the truth. Of the white fog incident of "Heart of Darkness," H. M. Daleski argues that

> the difficulties of pushing up the river and down into the unconscious are in part rendered in terms of sight, that artistic imperative of the preface [to *The Nigger of the "Narcissus"*]. Just before Kurtz's station is reached, the steamboat is enveloped in "a white fog, very warm and clammy, and more blinding than the night" [101], with the result that the travellers' eyes are 'of no

From *Studies in Short Fiction* 35 (1998): 373–386. © 1998 by Newberry College.

more use' to them than if they 'had been buried miles deep in a heap of cotton wool' [107]. (Daleski 52)

For Daleski, then, the white fog obscures sight, which Conrad had argued was his primary artistic goal: "to make you *see*" (Conrad, *Narcissus* xiv; original italics). Both Daleski and Said see the fog's obscuring quality as one of its primary purposes. The fog that appears in the white fog incident in "Heart of Darkness" does obscure—but it does more than merely obscure. In many ways, it actually clarifies certain issues for Marlow and his listeners (and perhaps his readers as well): the fog in fact uncovers—rather than obscures—issues concerning western civilization and western world view.

In narrating this event, Marlow discusses a number of subjects that seem to have little in common except that he happens to mention them at this point in the tale. Upon closer scrutiny, though, these images and events all repeat the same idea in various ways, ultimately leading to a view of the world in disorder and lacking any solid foundation; in effect, these images serve to generate such a world view. In the white fog incident, Marlow establishes a microcosm of human existence and cuts away the moorings that keep his listeners firmly anchored in the concrete, physical world, and by so doing he continually seeks to displace them from their comfortable environment. But more than this, Marlow removes the veneer of civilization that his listeners traditionally use to construct order for their existence. And so, whereas his listeners may assume that western civilization is based upon a solid and absolute foundation,[2] Marlow instead presents images of unexpectedness, absurdity, mystery, and chaos that serve to uncover a shifting and relative foundation for their world view. These images are in keeping with Conrad's own world, which Watt describes as "a panorama of chaos and futility, or cruelty, folly, vulgarity, and waste" (Watt 32). Image after image disorients Marlow and his listeners, forcing them to look at the possibility of a world of disorder and indifference, and although the individual images vary considerably, they work together to point toward such a world.[3] In the end, Marlow will come to see life as "that mysterious arrangement of merciless logic for a futile purpose" (150). The white fog incident is a precursor to that conclusion.

Throughout this episode concrete images and abstract ideas appear side by side as Marlow juxtaposes the physical world with the non-physical world and thus accentuates the differences between the two, requiring his listeners to deal with both the disparity between physical and non-physical worlds as well as the implications that arise as a consequence. Marlow opens the white fog incident by saying, "When the sun rose there was a white fog, very warm and clammy, and more blinding than the night. It did not shift or drive; it was just there, standing all round you like something solid" (101). The fog is "warm and clammy" and "solid," but, at the same time, it cuts off those on the steamboat from the outside world. Marlow emphasizes one sense (touch), while at the same moment removing another (sight). The fog also blinds: those on the steamboat can see nothing beyond their immediate physical being, and the fact that the fog is "more blinding than the night" inverts the traditional western view of light and dark (an inversion that occurs throughout the story). Marlow's listeners expect white to be a positive image, but, in fact, it is not because the white fog paralyzes them in a precarious position. As a result, from the beginning of this incident, the world of the story is played off against the world of his listeners, and a disparity appears. But lest his listeners think only the fog keeps them from the western concept of an orderly universe, Marlow continues:

> At eight or nine, perhaps, [the fog] lifted as a shutter lifts. We had a glimpse of the towering multitude of trees, of the immense matted jungle, with the blazing little ball of the sun hanging over it—all perfectly still—and then the white shutter came down again, smoothly, as if sliding in greased grooves. (101)

In addition to reminding his listeners about the "blinding" fog, upon its lifting, Marlow mentions "the immense matted jungle"—quite literally the wild and chaotic growth that contrasts with the seemingly orderly surroundings in which Marlow tells his tale.

With the fog rolling in again and covering the wilderness, Marlow's listeners encounter one of the most important images in the scene: "I ordered the chain, which we had begun to heave in, to be paid out again" (101). The chain here is a synecdoche for the anchor, and the image of the anchor will appear intermittently—at significant junctures—throughout the white fog incident. For those aboard, the anchor is solid and real: the mooring to hold the steamboat in place, but also a metaphor for the moorings westerners set up to try to understand the world around them. Conrad remarks elsewhere, "The anchor is an emblem of hope" (Conrad, *Mirror* 18).[4] But this image carries an unexpected quality in that Marlow presents an image whose symbolic referent—the moorings that maintain western world view—does not appear immediately. At this point, Marlow leaves a gap that he will not fill in till later. Not until a page or so later do Marlow's listeners encounter these metaphorical moorings. Therefore, Marlow in a sense forces them to listen backwards, an experience alien and unexpected, since what his listeners expect is a chronological narrative that follows the western concept of a linear progression of time.

Unexpectedness enters the narrative at other junctures as well. In fact, during this episode Marlow often narrates unexpected ideas and events. Based on their individual and cultural experience, as well as their knowledge of the external world, Marlow's listeners expect and predict certain things, but these objects and ideas are continuously absent, while something else appears in their stead. These various anomalies are as surprising as they are frequent. Immediately after the chain image, Marlow remarks,

> Before it stopped running with a muffled rattle, a cry, a very loud cry, as of infinite desolation, soared slowly in the opaque air. It ceased. A complaining clamour, modulated in savage discords, filled our ears. The sheer unexpectedness of it made my hair stir under my cap. I don't know how it struck the others: to me it seemed as though the mist itself had screamed, so suddenly, and apparently from all sides at once, did this tumultuous and mournful uproar arise. (101–02)

In this passage, Conrad juxtaposes two sounds—one expected, the other unexpected. The expected rattle of the chain is interrupted by the unexpected cry. The ordinariness of the chain accentuates the unordinariness of the cry. Both appear vividly to the listeners' senses: the sound of the running chain is "muffled," while the sound of the cry is "loud." The concreteness of the senses, however, is mirrored by the abstraction of the words "infinite" and "soared" because "infinite" cannot be comprehended and a sound cannot "soar." The word "soared" is further displaced: not only is the cry described as soaring but soaring "slowly"; hence Marlow tries to make the abstract concrete and thus further accentuates its abstract quality. The cry's very desolation (a desolation implying loneliness, barrenness, and displacement) isolates those on the steamboat from this experience. Marlow's reaction to its unexpectedness is also a reaction to the fear involved, and this fear directly results from the cry's unknown quality. Even its cessation is unexpected, as the very brevity of the sentence indicates: "It ceased."

This cry then leads to a "complaining clamour," which also "stopped short." An unexpected absence of sound, which Marlow calls "appalling and excessive" (102), then replaces the unexpected explosion of sound, and this absence of sound also indicates the absence of meaning behind this "uproar." In other words, for Marlow, the unexpectedness of the sound and the unexpectedness of its absence are both inexplicable. The most important point in this passage, though, is the clear absurdity of Marlow's attributing the cry to "the mist itself" and saying that it came "apparently from all sides at once." Both statements are obvious impossibilities. These logical impossibilities then elicit an invocation of deity—the believed ultimate author of western order—as one of the pilgrims exclaims, "Good God!" (102). This invocation, along with the fact that a "pilgrim" exclaims it, juxtaposes the idea of religion with the immediate events. Believing westerners typically view deity as capable of transforming the inexplicable into the explicable, and the pilgrim's invocation specifically aims at combating the implied chaos of the events they experience. Such an invocation, though, does not combat the chaos, but only serves to accentuate it by invoking a deity who does nothing to alter their precarious situation in a wilderness indifferent to their very existence.

The pilgrim's dress also shows the absurdity of the situation: facing death and the unknown in pink pajamas and red whiskers (102). Besides this description's humor, it also has two other functions. First, in its very absurdity, the description emphasizes metonymically the absurdity of the characters' situation as a whole, which the Winchesters then complement because the men cannot even see to shoot (102). Second, the description of the pilgrim's dress and the specific brand of rifle are concrete facts and evidence of the sensory world. Following these concrete facts is an unreal description of the steamboat, so that Marlow again juxtaposes concrete and abstract:

> What we could see was just the steamer we were on, her outlines blurred as though she had been on the point of dissolving, and a misty strip of water, perhaps two feet broad, around her—and that was all. The rest of the world was nowhere, as far as our eyes and ears were concerned. Just nowhere. Gone, disappeared; swept off without leaving a whisper or a shadow behind. (102)

This passage is one of the most significant in the white fog incident. At this point in the narrative, Marlow completely severs the men from the concrete world. The rest of the world is gone, so the only reality is the steamer itself, which is human-made and hence not an organic part of the world to which the humans wish to belong. And although the steamer is real, even that which is most solid and concrete for them at that moment has "her outlines blurred as though she had been on the point of dissolving." The steamer too then is becoming unreal, and with it reality itself is disintegrating with perhaps only nothingness to remain.

The fact that this incident occurs on water further emphasizes the shifting nature of images and events in this scene. In *The Mirror of the Sea*, Conrad remarks that "the sea has never been friendly to man . . . He—man or people—who [puts] his trust in the friendship of the sea . . . is a fool!" (Conrad, *Mirror* 135).[5] Although Conrad speaks here specifically of the sea, much of what he says applies equally to any body of water. Water is always alien to human existence; human beings are intruders in its world. Water is a place of dangers both seen and unseen: the possibility of drowning exists (to which Marlow alludes shortly afterward [106]), as well as unseen dangers that might lie within its murky depths. Both dangers cause fear—again, a fear of the unknown and the unpredictable. But most important, the water indicates the shifting nature of the world around those on the steamer. The steamer is the only solid thing in this frame, moored by a single, small anchor on a river composed of constant change and flux. The steamer is an unnatural construct, an imposition of civilization on the wilderness. And, in a sense, it is out of place as well, since it is going upstream, against the river's flow. In fact, the very object that keeps the steamer in place—the anchor—removes them from the natural world and yet also keeps them alive. Marlow refers to the anchor again just after introducing the dissolving steamer image (Marlow "ordered the chain to be hauled in short" [102]), and, like the steamer, it too is an artificial artifact and therefore out of place in nature. The anchor unnaturally resists the flow of nature, helping to isolate the men from the natural world around them.

Just after this second reference to the anchor, Marlow begins to deal with larger philosophical issues; first the possibility of death appears: "'Will they attack?' whispered an awed voice. 'We will be all butchered in this fog,' murmured another. The faces twitched with the strain, the hands trembled slightly, the eyes forgot to wink" (102). The fear of death, the paradigmatic fear of the unknown, appears at this point, and the narrative shifts from the descriptive and metaphoric to the cosmic. Ultimately, these cosmic questions target the most important issues in the story. The metaphor of the anchor then represents the men's (and Marlow's listeners') "grip on existence," which Marlow calls "precarious" (104). That they could be attacked and killed so easily shows that their position is indeed tenuous, and therefore what seems so solid—the anchor—is in fact not so solid at all. Not just the idea of death is significant at this juncture of the tale; the meaning of human existence also comes to the forefront. To arrive at this question, Marlow first juxtaposes the white men with the black men and contrasts them. One of the most interesting contrasts is Marlow's comment on the Africans' conception of time: "I don't think a single one of them had any clear idea of time, as we at the end of countless ages have. They still belonged to the beginnings of time—had no inherited experience to teach them, as it were" (103).[6]

Marlow points to one of the unique inventions of western civilization: chronological time. Chronological, or linear time, has as its primary feature discrete beginnings and endings to events, as well as specific reference points along the way. In addition to these features is the ability to differentiate one segment of time from another. In this way, westerners see time as progressing from one point to the next. This concept of time, however, is antithetical to natural, or cyclical time, in which beginnings and endings are relative and any points in between are shifting because cyclical time constantly turns back upon itself. In other words, in linear time, it is possible, for instance, to point specifically to the beginning of a month or its end or some point in between. In cyclical time, though, such reference points are not possible; for example (to take a roughly analogous time unit), in the cycle of the moon, it is possible to point to a new moon or a full moon, but it is not possible to determine which begins and which ends the cycle, since the cycle repeats itself over and over again without differentiating one cycle from another. The same could be said of the seasons: winter leads to spring which leads to summer which leads to fall which leads to winter, which leads to spring, and so on. Therefore, the fact that the Africans are unaware of Marlow's concept of time indicates that they do not function in linear time and hence have a different world view. In a sense, they exist in a different world from that of the westerners.

Besides the perceptual difference between the Europeans and the Africans, Marlow also comments on their physical differences:

> The whites, of course greatly discomposed, had besides a curious look of being painfully shocked by such an outrageous row. The others [the Africans] had an alert, naturally interested expression; but their faces were essentially quiet, even those of the one or two who grinned as they hauled at the chain. Several exchanged short, grunting phrases, which seemed to settle the matter to their satisfaction. (103)

The first thing Marlow mentions is the difference in composure, which leads to another reference to the anchor. But Marlow then goes on to emphasize the difference in their dress: "Their headman, a young broad-chested black, severely draped in dark-blue fringed cloths, with fierce nostrils and his hair all done up artfully in oily ringlets, stood near me" (103). The description thus becomes one of marked specificity and vividness, emphasizing the concrete. A few lines later, however, Marlow then refers again to the abstract as embodied in the image of fog (he "looked out into the fog" [103]). More than this, though, Marlow reveals the most distinct difference between the two groups—ethics: "'Catch 'im,' he [the head cannibal] snapped, with a bloodshot widening of his eyes and a flash of sharp teeth—'catch 'im. Give 'im to us.' 'To you, eh?' I asked; 'what would you do with them?' 'Eat 'im!' he said, curtly, and, leaning his elbow on the rail, looked out into the fog in a dignified and profoundly pensive attitude" (105).

The idea of cannibalism is so wholly removed from western civilized values that it serves as the perfect image to exemplify the contrast between the cultures, but in illuminating this contrast, it also brings to the forefront both modes of living—the civilized and the uncivilized. And at this same moment, Marlow points out the disturbing logic of the cannibals' request: it "occurred to me that he and his chaps must be very hungry: that they must have been growing increasingly hungry for at least this month past" (103). The cannibals are hungry, and therefore if they catch an attacker, they intend to eat him. Marlow immediately juxtaposes this perfectly logical reasoning with the attitude of civilization as symbolized by the cannibals' employment contract: "a piece of paper written over in accordance with some farcical law or other made down the river, it didn't enter anybody's head to trouble how they would live" (103). Marlow then remarks of the cannibals' wages that the trading company

> had given them every week three pieces of brass wire, each about nine inches long; and the theory was they were to buy their provisions with that currency in river-side villages. You can see how *that* worked. There were either no villages, or the people were hostile, or the director ... didn't want to stop the steamer for some more or less recondite reason. So, unless they swallowed the wire itself, or made loops of it to snare the fishes with, I don't see what good their extravagant salary could be to them. I must say it was paid with a regularity worthy of a large and honourable trading company. (104; original italics)

Their salary of brass wire, which is completely useless to the cannibals, reflects the absurdity of the contractual payment schedules (another example of western linear time). Consequently, cannibalism, one of the furthest removed and most abhorrent actions to western civilization, becomes more logical than the actions of civilization. And the orderly nature of the payment (the company's fulfillment of a contract) and the fact that the company pays it in an orderly manner (faithfully when due) appear to be an absurd imposition of order on this world. This fact then echoes other aspects of western civilization that appear here and elsewhere in the story, as each appearance of western civilization becomes for Marlow's listeners either absurd or incongruous in the African wilderness.[7]

The disturbing logic of the cannibals' situation, though, is superseded by the ultimate image of unexpectedness and inexplicability for Marlow:

> Why in the name of all the gnawing devils of hunger they didn't go for us—they were thirty to five—and have a good tuck-in for once, amazes me now when I think of it. They were big powerful men, with not much capacity to weigh consequences, with courage, with strength.... And I saw that something restraining, one of those human secrets that baffle probability, had come into play there. (104)

Among the many unexpected things that occur, Marlow encounters the most unexpected event in this part of the white fog incident. The cannibals' restraint is logically inexplicable. Marlow has tried to impose his own western perception of the world onto the cannibals' perception and as a result cannot understand their reasoning. He lists possibilities: "Restraint! What possible restraint? Was it superstition, disgust, patience, fear—or some kind of primitive honour?" (105). Marlow rejects all of these reasons:

> No fear can stand up to hunger, no patience can wear it out, disgust simply does not exist where hunger is; and as to superstition, beliefs, and what you may call principles, they are less than chaff in a breeze. Don't you know the devilry of lingering starvation, its exasperating torment, its black thoughts, its sombre and brooding ferocity? Well, I do. It takes a man all his inborn strength to fight hunger properly. It's really easier to face bereavement, dishonour, and the perdition of one's soul—than this kind of prolonged hunger. (105)

Marlow sees no rational explanation for the cannibals' restraint. Daleski comments, "The cannibal crew thus posit a capacity for the ultimate abandon of utter savagery at the same time as they exemplify the innate restraint that Marlow considers the only effective safeguard of civilized behaviour" (Daleski 65). The cannibals are at once both the antithesis and the paradigm of civilization: "And these chaps, too, had no earthly reason for any kind of scruple. Restraint! I would just as soon have expected restraint from a hyena prowling amongst the corpses of a battlefield" (105). In the image of the cannibals' restraint, Marlow effectually dismantles western civilized views because the restraint the cannibals exhibit is precisely what the Europeans lack throughout the story. Consequently, the cannibals in a sense act more civilized than do the Europeans. Marlow thus presents his listeners with an "enigma" without an answer:

> But there was the fact facing me—the fact dazzling, to be seen, like the foam on the depths of the sea, like a ripple on an unfathomable enigma, a mystery greater—when I thought of it—than the curious, inexplicable note of desperate grief in this savage clamour that had swept by us on the river-bank, behind the blind whiteness of the fog. (105)

Marlow describes this strange paradox as "a ripple on an unfathomable enigma." The ripple is a dual indicator; on the general level, it points to two things: something unexpected and something beneath the surface—but to the seaman Marlow, a ripple is also a sign of danger. A few lines before the beginning of the white fog incident, the men stop for the night because

Marlow says, "I could also see suspicious ripples at the upper end of the reach" (101). Therefore, this "ripple on a unfathomable enigma" indicates danger, a danger to western world view; it lurks just under the surface, the veneer of order that civilization has imposed, and threatens to run them aground, so that the danger to the westerners' physical beings (cannibalism) also represents the analogous danger to their psychological beings (chaos). The unexpected quality of the cannibals' restraint then is dangerous because it has no logical foundation. In this way, the principles and values of western society against which Marlow compares the cannibals' restraint also come under scrutiny; just as there seems to be no reason for the cannibals' restraint, Marlow also implies that if the roles were reversed, it would seem equally illogical to exercise restraint because restraint at such a point of hunger would seem absurd. Even besides this absurdity, by simply juxtaposing the actions of the cannibals and the principles of civilization, the principles come into question and consequently appear arbitrary. At this crucial juncture, explicit reference to the fog drifts back again into the narrative. The inexplicable nature of the cannibals' actions and the questionable foundation of western civilization end this passage shrouded in the irony of the fog's "blind whiteness" (105).

Marlow then shifts from the cosmically inexplicable to the specifically inexplicable, and this shifting from cosmic to specific continues to permeate Marlow's narrative, suggesting a tie between the two. For instance, Marlow says, "Two pilgrims were quarrelling in hurried whispers as to which bank. 'Left.' 'No, no; how can you? Right, right, of course'" (106). The pilgrims' quarrel has two purposes: it accentuates the disorientation of all those on the steamer (a metaphor for the cosmic disorientation of Marlow and his listeners), and this disorientation makes the whole conversation absurd. The point they argue is moot, and thus their discussion is useless as well. The narrative then shifts back again to the cosmic. First, as it does so often in this incident, the idea of death appears (in the pilgrims' concern as to which bank conceals the threat of attack and in the manager's reference to the possibility of Kurtz's being dead). And, of course, with death in general, but particularly when the death concerns an acquaintance (Kurtz), comes the question of the meaning of death and by comparison the meaning of life as well. The relationship of human beings to the universe, specifically whether civilization represents an ordered universe or is merely a construct imposed on the wilderness, is Marlow's primary concern. As a result, Marlow shifts subtly from references to death to questions of life through his seemingly innocuous assessment of the manager as "just the kind of man who would wish to preserve appearances" (106). (Actually, a disembodied "voice" rather than the man himself speaks to Marlow.) The manager represents, more so perhaps than any other character in the scene, the paradigmatic product of western civilization in his commitment to order: "he could keep the routine going" (74). The manager's wishing to preserve appearances (wishing to keep things in order) is apparent throughout the story, and as noted earlier, this same mentality governs the cannibals' salary of brass wire (which is equally absurd). But more than this, the surface appearance the manager wishes to preserve is a metonym for the rest of civilized order, and, just in case his listeners miss the point, Marlow then underscores it by pronouncing: "That was his restraint" (106). Marlow thereby forces his listeners back to the restraint of the cannibals and to the principles of civilization and invites them to see these principles as similarly absurd.

At the height of the appearance of these cosmic issues, the final specific reference to the anchor appears, but where we would expect the word "anchor," or even the synecdoche of the chain, Marlow only implies the anchor to his listeners: "I knew, and he knew, that it was impossible [to continue up the river]. Were we to let go our hold of the bottom, we would be absolutely in the air—in space" (106). At this reference to the anchor, complete physical isolation occurs. Marlow moves the men on the steamboat out of the intrusive (water) and into the impossible (space). Most important, though, the physical anchor once again represents a metaphorical anchor. In this way, Marlow portrays the men as completely disoriented, both physically and psychologically, and, like the physical "hold on the bottom," should the men let go of their metaphorical "hold of the bottom" (that is their faith in a western cosmology of an orderly universe), they would be psychologically "in space" as well. This in fact becomes Kurtz's end; Marlow later remarks, "I had to deal with a being to whom I could not appeal in the name of anything high or low. . . . There was nothing either above or below him, and I knew it. He had kicked himself loose of the earth" (144).

With this physical and psychological disorientation goes the threat of danger and death and the cosmic questions that come with it:

> We wouldn't be able to tell where we were going to—whether up or down stream, or across—till we fetched against one bank or the other,—and then we wouldn't know at first which it was. Of course I made no move. I had no mind for a smash-up. You couldn't imagine a more deadly place for a shipwreck. Whether drowned at once or not, we were sure to perish speedily in one way or another. (106)

The danger represented in this statement leads to the formal and ritualistic conversation between Marlow and the manager: "'I authorize you to take all the risks,' he [the manager] said, after a short silence. 'I refuse to take any,' I said shortly; which was just the answer he expected. . . . 'Well, I must defer to your judgment. You are captain,' he said, with marked civility" (106). This conversation is absurd in its uselessness, especially in the context of what precedes it. But for the manager, everything must be done in the correct order and customary manner. (The anchor is again in the background, with which the manager authorizes Marlow to "take all the risks" by hauling it in.) In this conversation, Marlow presents his listeners with yet another example of the order of western civilization, which continues to appear more and more out of place and absurd. The fog then floats again into the narrative (Marlow "looked into the fog" [106]), and the absurdity of the situation finishes with Marlow's statement (which turns it all into fantasy): "The approach to this Kurtz grubbing for ivory in the wretched bush was beset by as many dangers as though he had been an enchanted princess sleeping in a fabulous castle" (106).

Lest his listeners assume, though, that the absurdity and displacement affects merely the Europeans, Marlow displaces the Africans as well. Earlier, Marlow displaced the cannibals on the steamer remarking that they "were as much strangers to that part of the river as we, though their homes were only eight hundred miles away" (102–03). Their displacement appears most clearly in the fact that they cannot spend their salary because some of the people on the river are hostile to them. Just as the Europeans do not belong here, neither do the cannibals. Furthermore, Marlow also displaces the Africans on shore: "I did not think they would attack, for several obvious reasons. The thick fog was one. If they left the bank in their canoes they would get lost in it, as we would be if we attempted to move" (106–07). Marlow makes clear that the fog encompasses them all; not only are the Europeans and cannibals on the steamer displaced from the rest of the world, but also the Africans on shore (who would seem to be so much a part of the setting) would be displaced from the concrete world were they to let go of their "hold on the bottom," as it were, and so their moorings are as tenuous as those of everyone else in the story (as becomes clear later when Kurtz leaves them). Marlow then mentions the fog again, thereby reinforcing the human world's metaphorical displacement from the natural world. He further reinforces this idea, referring to the "impenetrable" (both actual and metaphorical) wilderness. Using such terms as "unexpected" and "unrestrained," Marlow again (unsuccessfully) attempts to explicate the meaning of the cry that was heard at the beginning of the white fog incident.

The final paragraph of the white fog incident synthesizes all that has come before; the narrative reaches a climax in its threat to rationality: "You should have seen the pilgrims stare! They had no heart to grin, or even to revile me: but I believe they thought me gone mad—with fright, maybe" (107). This reference to madness epitomizes all that has preceded because madness is the ultimate form of chaos. Inexplicable, unpredictable, and illogical, it is the paradigm of a world at odds with the western cosmology of

Marlow's listeners—but such is the world of "Heart of Darkness." Marlow encapsulates the entire incident by rolling the fog into the forefront once again, describing it—in a sense an intangible—in tangible terms ("a heap of cotton wool . . . choking, warm, stifling" [107]), and leaving the characters in the story in a "dream-sensation" (105), displaced from the concrete world. Marlow's introducing the fog again to close out this episode circumscribes the entire event. The last and most encompassing aspect of the white fog incident is that the final few images bring the scene full circle to where it started. It began with a palpable, blinding fog; a chaotic jungle; an anchor; desolate, inexplicable images; and the Africans. Similarly, Marlow ends by reiterating all of these images, encircled at last by the fog, so that the entire incident becomes the final image of indeterminacy in the narrative, gathering itself into the form of a circle—a circle of fog. This circle then becomes antithetical to a western cosmology that wishes to see things in terms of the linear and chronological as opposed to the cyclical and non-chronological. The linear allows reference points from which to organize; the cyclical does not. As a result, the cyclicality of the wilderness supplants the linearity of western cosmology. The world has become for Marlow at once more clear and less clear because of his experience. He better understands the world, but in understanding it he learns it is more incomprehensible than he had imagined. It is a world that, as Conrad puts it elsewhere, "seems to be mostly composed of riddles" (Conrad, Mirror ix). Thus the men enter and exit the fog cut off from the external world, and during the white fog incident, the displacement from the concrete that they experience serves as an extended metaphor for human existence, in which, in the world of "Heart of Darkness," there is only the immediate because there is no transcendent.

Notes

1. See, for example, "Heart of Darkness" (45), "An Outpost of Progress" (*Tales of Unrest* 115–17), *Lord Jim* (398–403), and "The Tale" (*Tales of Hearsay* 67–69).

2. Christopher GoGwilt and others have correctly argued that the West is not a single concept but rather various concepts put forward at different times for different reasons (see *Invention of the West*, especially 15–42). In "Heart of Darkness," however, Conrad seems to focus on a popularized and monolithic view of western civilization that saw its foundation in absolute truths.

3. Watt remarks that Conrad "belonged to the first generation that had not felt supported by the traditional view of man's flattering eminence in the history, as well as the design, of the cosmos" (154).

4. See also *Mirror* 15. Said echoes this sentiment: "[T]he sailor is aware that an anchor is one of the emblems of hope and rest" (151).

5. Compare also Conrad's comment a few pages later concerning "[t]he cynical indifference of the sea to the merits of human suffering and courage" (141).

6. In "An Outpost of Progress," the narrator makes a similar statement: "Those fellows [Africans], having engaged themselves to the Company for six months (without having any idea of a month in particular and only a very faint notion of time in general), had been serving the cause of progress for upwards of two years" (100).

7. Other examples of western ideas and artifacts appearing absurd or out of place in the African wilderness include the gunboat "firing into a continent" (62), the "objectless blasting" (64), the hole with the broken drainpipes (65–66), the dress of the company's chief accountant (67), and the stout man with moustaches trying to put out a fire by fetching water in a small pail with a hole in the bottom (76).

Works Cited

Conrad, Joseph. "Heart of Darkness." *Youth and Two Other Stories*. Garden City, New York: Doubleday, 1928. 45–162.

———. *Lord Jim*. Garden City, New York: Doubleday, 1928.

———. *The Mirror of the Sea*. Garden City, New York: Doubleday, 1928.

———. *The Nigger of the "Narcissus"*. Garden City, New York: Doubleday, 1928.

———. "An Outpost of Progress." *Tales of Unrest*. Garden City, New York: Doubleday, 1928. 86–117.

———. "The Tale." *Tales of Hearsay*. Garden City, New York: Doubleday, 1928. 59–81.

Daleski, H. M. *Joseph Conrad: The Way of Dispossession*. London: Faber, 1977.

GoGwilt, Christopher. *The Invention of the West: Joseph Conrad and the Double-Mapping of Europe and Empire*. Stanford, California: Stanford UP, 1995.

Said, Edward W. *Joseph Conrad and the Fiction of Autobiography*. Cambridge, Massachusetts: Harvard UP, 1966

Watt, Ian. *Conrad in the Nineteenth Century*. Berkeley: U of California P, 1979.

PERICLES LEWIS

"His Sympathies Were in the Right Place": Heart of Darkness *and the Discourse of National Character*

The Englishman who tells the story of Joseph Conrad's *Heart of Darkness* (1899), and the four who listen to it, do not consider it a particularly English story. The primary narrator does not repeat for it what he has already said in "Youth" of another of Marlow's tales: "This could have occurred nowhere but in England, where men and sea interpenetrate."[1] The action of *Heart of Darkness* takes place in "the centre of a continent"—Africa—and its main actors are employees of a European company, "a Continental concern."[2] Marlow comments that "all Europe contributed to the making of Kurtz" (p. 50), the novel's central figure, and most later critics have followed Marlow's lead in considering Kurtz's story one of European depravities, with little special reference to England. Chinua Achebe has criticized Conrad's vision of "Africa as a metaphysical battlefield devoid of all recognizable humanity, into which the wandering European enters at his peril"; while C. P. Sarvan, from the opposing camp, suggests that Conrad condemns the "representative[s] of civilized Europe" in Africa.[3]

Yet England has a special role to play in this story about the relations between Europe and Africa. Edward W. Said has suggested that Conrad's "two visions" allowed him to castigate "Belgian rapacity" while finding in "British rationality" the potential for a redemption of the imperialist project.[4] Eloise Knapp Hay, however, argues that "it seems the major burden of the

From *Nineteenth-Century Literature* 53, no. 2 (September 1998): 211–244. ©1998 by The Regents of the University of California.

51

story to reveal what Marlow has failed to see—that England is in no way exempt" from responsibility for imperialist outrages.[5] Yet Conrad's attitude toward English imperialism is more complex than either Said or Hay has suggested. England symbolizes both the ideal of efficient, liberal imperialism worshiped by Kurtz's "gang of virtue" (p. 28) and the sense of common purpose shared by the friends aboard the *Nellie*. The brooding gloom of Africa hovers over England too, and it is for this reason that the novel has become one of the most famous examples of "the ambivalence of colonial discourse."[6] Marlow tells his story in an effort to stave off this darkness by explaining his own behavior in Africa in ethical terms. Yet his inability to give a rational account of his attachment to Kurtz points to the power that Kurtz's many appeals to England and Englishness have over Marlow. It suggests that Marlow's ethical framework fails to account adequately for a mysterious "hidden something" ("Youth," p. 29), the power of national character that works on Marlow without his realizing it.

The contemporary crisis of liberal nationalism plays itself out in Marlow's problematic attempts to justify his actions in the Congo and especially his loyalty to Mr. Kurtz. Both Marlow and Conrad seem eager to defend the idea of England, which they associate with the values of a liberal, civilized society: "efficiency," "liberty," "sincerity of feeling," "humanity, decency, and justice."[7] Marlow is careful to distinguish the efficient and humane English, who rule by law and get "some real work" done in their possessions (p. 13), from the other European imperialists, who plunder their dependencies purely for their own material advantage while treating the natives indiscriminately as "enemies" and "criminals" (p. 20).

In the 1890s the values of English liberalism were under attack on two fronts. On the one hand deterministic theories of national character, such as that hinted at by the Company Doctor, suggested that the values Conrad associated with the "idea" of England were the result not of shared devotion to common beliefs (of what we today would call "English culture") but of essential physical differences among the various nationalities, of the brute fact of "Englishness." On the other hand the growth of universalistic, democratic, and socialist politics, represented in the novel by Kurtz, threatened to level the cultural differences—the specifically English institutions and specifically English character—that Victorian liberals had prized. The Rights of Man threatened to efface "the rights of Englishmen."[8] Michael Tratner and Michael Levenson have each recently explored the responses of English modernism to the threats posed by such mass movements to the values of liberal individualism.[9] Within liberal politics the two traditional strands, Whig and Radical, had reemerged in the conflict between Unionists and supporters of Irish Home Rule in the 1880s. Among political theorists the old Whiggish defense of specifically English liberties was to give way on the one hand to the crasser forms of social Darwinism and on the other to the New Liberalism with its internationalist aspirations. *Heart of Darkness* enacts the conflict within English liberalism at the turn of the century between a traditional Whig defense of liberal values as reflections of the English national character not necessarily suitable for other nations and a growing aspiration toward a universalistic, international democracy.

Conrad shows the impasse that English liberal nationalism has reached as it confronts the results of imperialism and social Darwinism. Marlow's perplexity suggests that English liberalism cannot offer an adequate account of the role of cultural differences in shaping political beliefs. Marlow senses the threat posed to his Victorian English liberal values, his ethos, by both the Company's vulgar materialism and Kurtz's unworldly idealism.[10] He rejects the Doctor's biological theory of national character, but he cannot hold out for long against Kurtz's appeals to "moral ideas" (p. 33), laden as they are with claims on Marlow's English sympathies. In the Congo Marlow faces a "choice of nightmares," and he chooses Kurtz, although he cannot say why.

Kurtz offers Marlow a vision of internationalist politics that appeals, strangely enough, to Marlow's specifically English values. The narrative alludes to the symbolic importance of England in motivating many elements of Kurtz's savage enterprise. Kurtz, having "been educated partly in England," claims to admire English ideas: "as he was good enough to say himself—his sympathies were in the right place" (p. 50). Indeed, Marlow tells his listeners that the "wraith" of Kurtz chooses to relate his story to Marlow "because it could speak English to me." "Sympathy" with the enlightened English mode of imperialism marks Kurtz and his associates off from the Company's other employees, making them part "of the new gang—the gang of virtue," who see themselves, according to the brickmaker, as "emissar[ies] of pity, and science, and progress, and devil knows what else" (p. 28). Whereas most of the other employees come from various countries in continental Europe, Kurtz and his two followers with non-African blood have strong biological or emotional connections to England: Kurtz himself has a "half-English" mother (p. 50) and his followers are "an English half-caste clerk" and a Russian who has "served some time in English ships" (pp. 34, 54). None of these Kurtzians, however, is purely English. They are all products of biological or intellectual miscegenation: quarter-English, half-English, or merely anglophile. They suggest Englishness gone wrong, a misinterpretation of liberal English values. It is Kurtz's imperfect Englishness that makes him such an extremist in the application of the putatively English values of pity, science, progress, and virtue.

Marlow himself appears to be the Company's first purely English employee. The Company Doctor, who measures Marlow's cranium "in the interests of science" before he leaves for Africa and asks him in French whether there has ever been any madness in his family, excuses himself. "Pardon my questions, but you are the first Englishman coming under my observation" (p. 15). Marlow's Englishness plays an important part in his Congo experience, differentiating him from all of the other Company employees, linking him to his listeners on the *Nellie*, and eventually serving as the basis for an intimate connection between him and Kurtz. Kurtz and his admirer the Russian harlequin continually address Marlow with attention to his nationality, thus "interpellating" him as an Englishman.[11] Marlow appears only half-aware of the extent to which his Englishness defines him for those he meets. He inhabits the identity of a representative Englishman uneasily, eager to appear instead as a cosmopolitan cynic. He assures the Company Doctor, who hints that nationality may determine character, that he is "not in the least typical" of his countrymen: "If I were, . . . I wouldn't be talking like this with you" (p. 15). The Doctor responds: "What you say is rather profound and probably erroneous."

The problem posed by the Company Doctor will come back to haunt Marlow's narration, for Marlow finds himself unable to describe his motives for his own actions in Africa. He continually refers to the inexplicability of his attachment to Kurtz: "It is strange how I accepted this unforeseen partnership, this choice of nightmares forced upon me in the tenebrous land invaded by these mean and greedy phantoms" (p. 67). He can never quite adequately explain why he chooses Kurtz's nightmare over the Company's, why he admits to being Kurtz's "friend," or why he is willing to be considered a member "of the party of 'unsound method'" (p. 67). Yet this choice is the central ethical problem of the story's climactic final section.

One notable force acts on Marlow, apparently without his realizing it. Throughout the story, and especially in the second installment (in which Marlow recounts his meeting with Kurtz), appeals to his nationality gradually draw Marlow into the "gang of virtue." Marlow's "choice of nightmares" shows the importance to him not only of Kurtz's claim to represent liberal English values but also of the more basic appeals to "partnership," "brotherhood," "friendship," and "sympathy" made by Kurtz and his ally the Russian harlequin, always on the basis of their shared association with things English. Marlow never says that Kurtz's connection to England forms one of his attractions and makes him, in the words of *Lord Jim*, "one of us,"[12] yet the many references to Marlow's Englishness provide a meaningful explanation for his choosing Kurtz over the Company, a choice for which Marlow himself cannot account. During his nightmarish progression up the Congo, whenever something reminds him of England, Marlow discovers a moment of truth or "reality" among the many lies and illusions of the Company. Whatever appeals to his basic humanity or to his English nationality, whatever is "meaningful," "natural," or "true," draws Marlow to Kurtz's side in the inexplicable "choice of nightmares."

Ever more frequent allusions to England and Englishness in the story's second installment suggest that Marlow has failed to see how his very Englishness is drawing him deeper into Kurtzian depravity. The references to England create a structural pattern of irony in which Marlow's subjective perceptions (his belief in the universal validity of English values) fail to match his objective situation (the contingency and perhaps even hypocrisy on which these values depend).[13] Marlow persistently sees more than the "typical" Englishman would see, but then he turns out to be more typically English in his blindnesses than he would have expected. His dual role as participant in and teller of his story makes his own account of the motivations for his "choice of nightmares" suspect. Marlow tells his story to four English friends, and its "spokenness" is crucial, for it suggests the process by which Marlow attempts to make sense of what he has done. He seems to believe that "a man's character is his fate" ("*ēthos anthropōi daimōn*"),[14] and he tends to explain the events of his story in ethical terms, from the perspective of a participant.[15] He accounts for the various actions he describes by reference to the unique moral characteristics of the actors involved, particularly to their possession or lack of "restraint," "innate strength," or "character." Marlow makes many remarks of a sociological or anthropological nature on the Company, its employees, and the Africans, yet he seems unable to grasp completely the ways in which powerful cultural forces have determined his own character (his *ethos*). For example, he attempts to account to himself for both Mr. Kurtz's actions and his own primarily on the grounds of morality and free will; he is eager to see the "restraint" exercised by the cannibals on board his steamer in the Congo as akin to the restraint of civilized Englishmen; and he wants to believe that a good character can be measured by universally applicable standards, and thus that *ethos* is itself a universal measure rather than merely a product of accident.

Ironically enough, it is by an appeal to Englishness that Kurtz attempts to convince Marlow of the validity of Kurtz's own internationalist goals. Whereas Kurtz and Marlow are both attracted by the possibility of an international politics based on virtue and efficiency, Conrad seems to suggest that the very values they affirm are so dependent on a particular cultural framework as to be unsuitable for export. Perhaps partly because of his mixed parentage, Kurtz has carried his putatively English values to un-English extremes. It is Marlow's very susceptibility to the claims of "virtue," conditioned by his own Englishness, that makes him capable of being swayed by Kurtz's universalist appeal. What Kurtz presents as universally valid ideals—"pity, and science, and progress"—turn out to be terribly culturally specific. Conrad presents the reader with the material for a sociological perspective on Marlow's and Kurtz's actions in which this paradox becomes apparent: the novel is a written document that contains Marlow's spoken story in crystallized form as well as the primary narrator's observations of Marlow.

This written document, by showing Marlow from the outside, suggests the influence on him of apparently irrational cultural forces. In the framing of Marlow's narrative, the novel takes on its significance as the story of the national idea, for it is the primary narrator who at the beginning of the novel apotheosizes the Thames as the river that has "known and served all the men of whom the nation is proud" and who at the end observes that "the tranquil waterway leading to the uttermost ends of the earth flowed sombre under an overcast sky—seemed to lead into the heart of an immense darkness" (pp. 8, 76). The written frame suggests the limits of Marlow's perspective, his inability to explain his own actions. It shows how forces beyond his control shape his action and his character: "I did not betray Mr. Kurtz—it was ordered I should never betray him—it was written I should be loyal to the nightmare of my choice" (p. 64). Yet unlike many realist novels of the nineteenth century, *Heart of Darkness* neither presents an omniscient narrator who can give a purely objective account of Marlow's character nor allows Marlow to achieve the final sort of maturity that would make all of his mistakes and uncertainties clear to him. At the end of the novel, recounting his lie to the Intended, Marlow will be just as baffled about his own motives as he was when he set out to tell the story. The reader is afforded no position outside culture. Indeed, the novel calls attention to the fact that it is written in English and that it tells the story of five Englishmen discussing far-off events. At key moments of the story Marlow points out that he speaks with most of the Company's employees in French: he must make sense in English terms of what seems a very foreign story.

Marlow's ethical discourse, based on his own free will, occasionally breaks down, and he seems to become aware of the possibility of a sociological explanation of his actions as determined by particular social and cultural forces. One such moment occurs after he proclaims his faith in the idea that redeems "the conquest of the earth": "What redeems it is the idea only. An idea at the back of it, not a sentimental pretence but an idea; and an unselfish belief in the idea—something you can set up, and bow down before, and offer a sacrifice to . . ." (p. 10). After the ellipsis, the primary narrator announces: "He [Marlow] broke off" (p. 11). Here Marlow glimpses the possibility that the idea he reveres may appear to his listeners as a type of cultural fetish, a product made by humans' own activities but worshiped by them as a god. He therefore breaks off uneasily, just as later in the story he will frequently cut short his narration while he attempts to think through the ethical consequences of his own or Kurtz's actions: "it is impossible to convey the life-sensation of any given epoch of one's existence—that which makes its truth, its meaning—its subtle and penetrating essence. It is impossible. We live, as we dream—alone . . ." (p. 30). Marlow's idiosyncratic mode of narration—his heavy foreshadowing and impressionistic accounts of his perceptions—calls attention to the possible inadequacy of his ethical explanation of events. It signals the development of a distinctively modern consciousness of the forces through which culture shapes character and of the inevitable lack of an Archimedean point from which to make either ethical or sociological judgments.[16] Marlow's perplexity results in part from a tension within his own liberal nationalism. Whereas he wishes to assert the universal validity of the values he embraces and associates with England, he also suspects that these values merely seem universal from a particular idiosyncratic worldview that is itself the product of historical accident. Marlow uneasily occupies the dual position of participant in and observer of English ideology.

It is the indeterminacy of Marlow's motivations that makes *Heart of Darkness* a crucial founding example of literary modernism. It is surely the case, as Conrad's critics have shown, that a variety of psychic, sexual, and social forces draw Marlow into his "choice of nightmares." Yet the story suggests that one of the most significant of the forces through which culture molds character is the mysterious power of nationality, that "hidden something" that works almost unnoticeably on Marlow and that he can never fully articulate. Scholars of Conrad's politics have developed two opposing accounts of his worldview, which I call the organicist-nationalist and the liberal-individualist. Avrom Fleishman, for example, attributes to Conrad three "guiding principles": "organic community, the work ethic, and the critique of individualism."[17] Yet Ian Watt rightly objects that Conrad held to "basic social attitudes which, though certainly not democratic, were in many ways deeply egalitarian and individualist" (p. 110). Conrad himself expressed sympathy with liberal politics, asserting for example that his mind "was fed on ideas, not of revolt but of liberalism of a perfectly disinterested kind, and on severe moral lessons of national misfortune."[18] He claimed in particular that England and the English system of government were uniquely well suited to the development of individual liberties. The fact that Conrad's primary political commitments were to a form of liberal individualism and to nationalism has been one source of the extended debates over his politics, largely because critics in the late twentieth century tend to see liberalism and nationalism as essentially contradictory systems of belief. However, a strong nationalistic current within English liberalism, from Edmund Burke to Leslie Stephen, had venerated English institutions as especially suited to the development of liberty and had even associated the unique character of English institutions with the unique character of the English people.[19] Conrad spoke the language of this English liberal nationalism, treating faith in the nation-state as the necessary corollary of a belief in the fundamentally egoistic and individualistic character of human nature.

Conrad expressed many of the concerns of Victorian liberal nationalists in a letter to R. B. Cunninghame Graham, written on 9 February 1899, the day after he sent his publisher the manuscript of the final two installments of *Heart of Darkness*. In this letter Conrad thanks Cunninghame Graham for his compliments on the first installment, which had recently appeared in *Blackwood's Magazine*, but warns him that in the remainder of the novel the "note struck" may no longer "[chime] in with [his] convictions."[20] Conrad's critics have studied this letter but have failed to make the connection between his comments on the novel he was just completing and the remainder of the letter, in which he draws attention to the centrality of "l'idée nationale," "une idée sans avénir," to his political worldview (*Collected Letters*, II, 159, 160).[21] Conrad attacks his friend's faith in social democracy and international fraternity: "I can not admit the idea of fraternity not so much because I believe it impracticable, but because its propaganda (the only thing really tangible about it) tends to weaken the national sentiment the preservation of which is my concern" (*Collected Letters*, II, 158). He argues that "l'idée nationale" is preferable to "l'idée démocratique" as the basis for a political system. As an alternative to international fraternity, he defends egoism and nationalism: "There is already as much fraternity as there can be—and that's very little and that very little is no good. What does fraternity mean. Abnegation—self-sacrifice means something. Fraternity means nothing unless the Cain–Abel business. That's your true fraternity.... C'est l'égoisme qui sauve tout—absolument tout—tout ce que nous abhorrons tout ce que nous aimons" (*Collected Letters*, II, 159).[22] Conrad says that "l'idée democratique est un très beau phantôme," in the service of "les ombres d'une eloquence qui est morte, justement par ce qu'elle n'a pas de corps (*Collected Letters*, II, 158–59)."[23] However, he defends the national idea by suggesting that at least it is "un principe défini" (*Collected Letters*, II, 159; "a definite principle"). Throughout this letter Conrad draws on a recurrent trope in English political thought that can be traced back, as Fleishman has noted, at least to Edmund Burke's response to the French Revolution: namely, the danger that democratic ideals of international fraternity will undermine the true source of solidarity in the shared national character.[24] Conrad argues, however, not (as Fleishman suggests) against individualism but in favor of nationalism as a form of super-individualism, which appeals to the egoistic impulses essential to human nature. Conrad's defense of "l'idée nationale" echoes many of Marlow's comments on social and political matters in *Heart of Darkness* and links them to the English liberal tradition and to the turning-point at which it had arrived by the 1890s.

Ultimately, Conrad's letter to Cunninghame Graham shows that as he was finishing *Heart of Darkness* Conrad was attempting to come to terms with the potential conflict between liberalism and nationalism. Throughout the nineteenth century the two forces had gone hand in hand, as liberal movements sought to replace multinational empires within Europe with self-governing nation-states. Conrad still wants to hold to the old faith in the national bond as the source of "sympathies" that can bind together free and equal individuals within an increasingly competitive and atomized liberal society, yet tendencies within both liberalism and nationalism threatened to destroy this faith. In particular, the principle of nationality could not be extended outside of Europe without threatening the interests of European imperialists.

The optimistic, liberal idea that a world of nation-states could embody the principles of freedom, equality, and justice had motivated the founding of the Congo Free State. In 1885 Henry M. Stanley had written:

> On the 14th of August, 1879, I arrived before the mouth of this river [the Congo] to ascend it, with the novel mission of sowing along its banks civilised settlements, to peacefully conquer and subdue it, to remould it in harmony with modern ideas into National States, within whose limits the European merchant shall go hand in hand with the dark African trader, and justice and law and order shall prevail, and murder and lawlessness and cruel barter of slaves shall for ever cease.[25]

The nation-state was to serve the liberal goals of rule by law and peaceful competition among individuals, and mid-Victorian liberals such as John Stuart Mill defended imperialism as a stage on the road to representative government and a world of liberal nation-states.[26] In the wake of Darwinism and the disillusionments of the scramble for Africa, however, nationalism and liberalism came increasingly to appear as opposed principles, with nationalists embracing theories of racial determinism and liberals looking toward a future of universal government.

In the letter to Cunninghame Graham, Conrad invokes a possessive-individualist psychology in the English empiricist vein when he writes that "l'homme est un animal méchant. Sa méchanceté doit être organisée" (*Collected Letters*, II, 159).[27] By reference to Cain and Abel ("that's your true fraternity") he suggests that the state of nature was no paradise. His defense of egoism suggests a Hobbesian understanding of the motivation for the formation of civil society in self-defense, or what might be called unenlightened self-interest. However, Conrad's appeals in the letter to "self-sacrifice," "abnegation," and "fidélité à une cause absolument perdue" ("fidelity to an absolutely lost cause") point to a more positive conception of human nature and society. For Conrad the "national sentiment" can cultivate these qualities by encouraging solidarity among individuals. This belief corresponds to the positive side of the English liberal tradition's conception of the nation-state. Far from endorsing the cash nexus as the sole desirable relationship among people, many late-Victorian liberals turned to the shared sense of nationhood as a source of forms of sociability that would mitigate the potentially antisocial effects of an economic and political system based on competition. They described such forms of sociability with words like "altruism," "sympathy," "character," "culture," and "civilization."[28] Like Burke and his many Victorian admirers, Conrad rejects the attempt to create a political system based purely on rationality and equality, but he suggests that in the context of a cohesive civil society, inspired by the idea of the nation, people are capable of overcoming their more brutish instincts and creating a meaningful social order.

Conrad alludes in the letter to his devotion to "une cause absolument perdue, à une idée sans avenir" (Collected Letters, II, 160). While he is referring in part specifically to the idea of Poland, he seems also to suspect that the idea of nationality in general is in danger of becoming outmoded. Conrad's faith in nationalism was shaped by his parents' involvement in the struggle for Polish nationhood, but he also applied his trust in the "national idea" to his adoptive motherland, England—and it was through the figure of Marlow that he explored the peculiarities of the English national character.

The two concerns that motivate Conrad's defense of the "national idea"—an individualist conception of human nature and an emphasis on the ways in which social institutions contained the potentially destructive impulses associated with individualism—became, in post-Darwinian England, the focus of a debate about the sources and nature of national character. Evolutionary thought encouraged many social thinkers to understand the characters of various peoples as resulting from the historical development of their cultures and institutions. These thinkers often expressed skepticism about the possibility of exporting English institutions, such as rule by law and representative government, to other nations. Almost all English liberals and other writers on the subject agreed that the English had a propensity for liberty that other nations lacked; the main source of disagreement was the question of whether people of other nationalities, from the French to Indians and Africans, could eventually benefit from English institutions and customs or whether elements of their "characters" made them permanently unsuitable for liberty. As George W. Stocking, Jr., has shown, among liberal political thinkers in particular the challenge posed by the evident diversity of national characters was to defend the traditional Enlightenment (and Christian) view that, despite the variety of human cultures, human nature was fundamentally one.[29]

Evolutionary thought had at first assisted liberals in making the case that even primitive cultures were capable of developing the character necessary for self-rule. Toward the end of the nineteenth century, however, the idea of national character began to harden in political discourse. Rather than referring to what the twentieth century has come to call "culture," national character increasingly meant what we today call "race."[30] Whereas Burke's primarily political conception of national character had emphasized the importance of English institutions, some of his later admirers attributed the unique character of English liberty not to England's constitutional arrangements but to the physical constitution of Englishmen. The claim that the English had a privileged national relationship with liberty eventually became part of chauvinist propaganda, exemplified by the argument that British imperialism derived from the "desire of spreading throughout the habitable globe all the characteristics of Englishmen—their energy, their civilization, their religion and their freedom."[31] Conrad's defense of England's conduct in the Boer War contains the distant echo of Burke's faith in "the rights of Englishmen": "That they [the Boers] are struggling in good faith for their independence cannot be doubted; but it is also a fact that they have no idea of liberty, which can only be found under the English flag all over the world."[32]

By the 1890s the discourse of national character faced a crisis. The growing eugenicist movement treated character as strictly a result of biological heredity. Eugenics already had a strong following in England by the time that Karl Pearson argued, in 1900, that in England "the feckless and improvident ... have the largest families ... at the expense of the nation's future.... [We] cannot recruit the nation from its inferior stocks without deteriorating our national character."[33] The notion of a distinctive national character in such theories implied the opposite of liberalism. Rather than foster the natural, progressive development of character through liberal institutions, eugenicists proposed forms of social engineering that would ensure the reproduction of the "superior stock" among the English. Traditional individualist and ethical notions of behavior were irrelevant to such projects. Some important, liberal Darwinists, such as T. H. Huxley in his lecture "Evolution and Ethics," objected to such uses of Darwinism, recognizing that the so called "evolution of society" was "a process of an essentially different character" from that of "the evolution of species."[34] Huxley argued that the ethical standards by which people in society decide how to act are and should be diametrically opposed to the processes by which the fittest survive in the state of nature, and that the development of human societies could no more be understood as the result of natural selection than could the growth of a highly cultivated garden (pp. 10–15).

From the perspective of the evolutionary social sciences, however, such a stance could not claim scientific validity; rather, it appeared to be a last-ditch effort to maintain the worn-out categories of liberal thought against the onslaught of a more rational biological determinism that seemed to hold the true key to history. Because of the continuing strength of positivism, social theory in late-Victorian England generally did not confront the problems of cultural relativism and pluralism or the intellectual limitations of biological determinism that concerned contemporary continental thinkers such as Durkheim and Weber and that H. Stuart Hughes describes in *Consciousness and Society* (pp. 278–335). As a result, the discourse of national character tended to fade into a strict determinism with distinctly pro-imperialist and authoritarian overtones. Meanwhile, on the political left, democrats and Fabian socialists generally maintained their faith in the rationality of human nature and paid relatively little attention to the problems of cultural difference and historicism that were associated with the notion of national character and its Burkean heritage.

Conrad is stuck between the two extremes of racial determinism and an unbounded faith in the universality of human nature; in *Heart of Darkness* he offers an almost allegorical account of the conflict between these two perspectives. What makes Conrad such a complex figure, however, is that he endorses neither racial determinism nor internationalist democracy but rather presents liberal values as the fragile products of historical accident that seem destined to develop successfully only in a particular cultural context.

Seen in part as the story of the "national idea," *Heart of Darkness* participates in contemporary debates about national character and the capacity of particular cultures for civilization and progress. One target of Conrad's critique, as Ian Watt has shown (pp. 147–68), is the extreme optimism of those advocates of progress, like Kurtz, who maintain a sort of mid-Victorian faith in the ultimate triumph of civilized values. *Heart of Darkness* describes a polarity between what Conrad in the letter to Cunninghame Graham calls "les ombres d'une eloquence qui est morte" (social democracy) and "un principe défini" (the nation). Kurtz exemplifies the internationalist attitude that Conrad criticized in Cunninghame Graham and his social-democratic friends. Kurtz's politics are populist rather than specifically social-democratic, since he has the character of a demagogue, as his colleague's comment to Marlow shows: "This visitor informed me Kurtz's proper sphere ought to have been politics 'on the popular side.... He would have been a splendid leader of an extreme party.... Any party.... He was an—an—extremist'" (p. 71).

Kurtz's vision of imperialism in the service of civilization has made him the favorite of "the International Society for the Suppression of Savage Customs." In the first lines of his report for this Society he wrote that "we whites ... 'must necessarily appear to them [savages] in the nature of supernatural beings.... By the simple exercise of our will we can exert a power for good practically unbounded'" (p. 50). Kurtz here echoes the most optimistic conclusions of the Enlightenment, such as Rousseau's claim that "he who could do everything would never do harm."[35] "This," says Marlow, "was the unbounded power of eloquence—of words—of burning noble words" (p. 50). Yet the optimism of Kurtz's opening paragraph seems to lead inexorably to the insanity of his postscript to the report: "Exterminate all the brutes!" (p. 51).[36] By believing in himself and his rationality alone, by abandoning the body and "kick[ing] himself loose of the earth" (p. 65), by serving "the shades of an eloquence that is dead," Kurtz has been led to a vision of himself as God—and this is in effect the mistake made, in Conrad's view, by the social democrats.[37] Conrad's defense of egoism as the basis of human society suggests that by recognizing the fact that selfish interests motivate our behavior, we can escape Kurtzian self-delusion.

While Conrad may be skeptical of the optimism of the Enlightenment, he does not embrace the opposite extreme within the Victorian debate over national character, namely the racial determinism that saw differences among various human societies as directly reflecting underlying biological differences among the races. The Company Doctor represents one pre-Darwinian variant of racial determinism, the polygenetic tradition that had produced such monuments of Victorian physical anthropology as Bernard Davis and Joseph Thurnam's *Crania Britannica* (1865).[38] The Doctor has a "little theory" that somehow correlates size of cranium, nationality, and ability to survive in Africa:

> "I always ask leave, in the interests of science, to measure the crania of those going out there.... Ever any madness in your family?.... It would be ... interesting for science to watch the mental changes of individuals on the spot, but.... I have a little theory which you Messieurs who go out there must help me to prove. This is my share in the advantages my country shall reap from the possession of such a magnificent dependency. The mere wealth I leave to others. Pardon my questions, but you are the first Englishman coming under my observation...." (p. 15)

Marlow rejects the application of a physical scientific theory of national character to his own case. The claim that merely physical characteristics differentiate the Englishman from other Europeans or from Africans seems to offend him because it does not leave room for the "idea" that redeems "the conquest of the earth." If this biological theory of national character were correct, Marlow senses, human autonomy would be a sham, for each person would pursue his or her own lusts without any enlightenment, driven on by material interest and without any moral purpose.[39] The Company's bureaucracy epitomizes such a potential future world, in which the social bond that makes the nation strong has been degraded to a pact among thieves for the distribution of the booty of imperialism. In a world dominated by a struggle among the races, the strongest race would win, regardless of ideals.

As Marlow observes near the beginning of the novel, "[the Romans] were conquerors, and for that you want only brute force—nothing to boast of, when you have it, since your strength is just an accident arising from the weakness of others" (p. 10). If the Doctor were right in attributing national character simply to biological difference, then all conquests would result from a similar "accident."

Marlow particularly dislikes the use of such "scientific" methods on himself, although the possibility that the Doctor suggests—that some fundamental racial difference, correlated with biological inheritance, shapes the actions of various national groups once they get to Africa—haunts him. On his trip up to the Central Station, Marlow makes "a speech in English with gestures" (p. 23) to the sixty Africans under his command, and when they continue to disobey him, he begins to doubt his own sanity and remembers his conversation with the Company Doctor: "'It would be interesting for science to watch the mental changes of individuals on the spot.' I felt I was becoming scientifically interesting" (p. 24). Marlow's admission that he himself could be "scientifically interesting" leaves open the possibility that the actions of the various characters in *Heart of Darkness* reflect such underlying racial differences. Yet Marlow rejects this mode of explanation. Kurtz's idealism about human nature, even carried to horrible extremes, seems more congenial to him than the crass materialism of the Company and its philosophical expression in the Doctor's "little theory." Other factors, apparently not understood by Marlow himself, seem to contribute to Marlow's choice, however, most notably a long series of appeals to his nationality made by Kurtz and the Russian harlequin. These factors also point to an understanding of human nature and politics that is different than either the racialism of the Company Doctor or the extreme historical optimism of Kurtz. For Conrad, cultural factors—speaking the same language, smoking the same tobacco, shared attitudes toward work—and the habits of mind associated with them play a fundamental part in the makeup of the individual. The success of a liberal political organization seems to depend for him on the fortuitous combination of such ineffable cultural factors.

The novel's opening pages establish two competing versions of a historical explanation of the cultural differences among various human societies, each inspired by the meeting of Marlow and his listeners aboard the *Nellie* and each suggesting an alternative explanation for the origins of noble sentiments in the idea of the nation. At first Conrad seems to be presenting a fairly conventional picture of the English nation—or at least its adult male middle class—as the embodiment of liberal ideals. Yet, as Hunt Hawkins pointed out in his lecture on "Conrad's Idea of Englishness," Conrad both "makes and unmakes" the idea of Englishness in his works. *Heart of Darkness* presents a competition among differing conceptions of precisely where

English greatness lies. The only cohesive community that the novel offers as an alternative to Kurtz's disembodied dreams is the friendship of the five men aboard the *Nellie*, the cruising yawl on which Marlow tells the stories of "Youth" and *Heart of Darkness*.

Conrad originally planned to have the first three Marlow stories appear together in a single volume, *"Youth: A Narrative" and Two Other Stories*,[40] beginning with the opening statement by the primary narrator of "Youth":

> This could have occurred nowhere but in England, where men and sea interpenetrate, so to speak—the sea entering into the life of most men, and the men knowing something or everything about the sea, in the way of amusement, of travel, or of bread-winning. (p. 3)

What "could have occurred nowhere but in England" is the gathering of Marlow and his four friends to share Marlow's story of his first command[41]—the same friends who later, aboard the *Nellie*, listen to his account of his journey to the Congo. "We all began life in the merchant service," the primary narrator of "Youth" observes; "Between the five of us there was the strong bond of the sea" (p. 3). At the beginning of *Heart of Darkness* he comments again: "Between us there was as I have already said somewhere, the bond of the sea" (p. 7). This "bond of the sea," forged in the merchant service, and the narrator's comment in "Youth" that in England "men and sea interpenetrate," suggest that the friendship of the five men has about it something typically English—that their society is a microcosm of the English nation, the island that another Conradian narrator describes as "A great ship! . . . A ship mother of fleets and nations! The great flagship of the race; stronger than the storms! and anchored in the open sea."[42] On board the *Nellie*, just a few miles from the open sea, at the gateway from England to the rest of the world, Marlow and his four listeners seem to carry on this function of symbolizing the English nation. The nation appears as a bond among adult men who are all on relatively equal terms with one another precisely because, as in the English parliament of the time, women, the lower classes, children, and of course foreigners are excluded and assumed to be inferior.

The primary narrator tells the first, unabashedly heroic version of the collective story. The Thames, resting "unruffled at the decline of day after ages of good service done to the race that peopled its banks," causes the five men on the *Nellie* to "evoke the great spirit of the past," a history of conquest and commerce that, without any conscious plan on the part of men but as if by divine providence, has spread around the world "spark[s] from the sacred fire" (p. 8). The narrator offers a Whiggish interpretation of English history as running in an unabated upward movement from the Elizabethans to the

Victorians, spurred on by commerce and conquest. To Marlow, however, the process of civilization appears as a mere flash of light intervening between prolonged periods of darkness. Only after describing the times when Britons were savages and the wilderness exercised "the fascination of the abomination" on the first Roman conquerors does Marlow, as if embarrassed, distinguish himself and his English listeners from the Romans (and from the pre-Roman Britons as well): "Mind, none of us would feel exactly like this. What saves us is efficiency—the devotion to efficiency" (p. 10). Marlow goes on to utter his famous statement about the idea that redeems "the conquest of the earth." The narrator's "great spirit of the past" transforms itself into Marlow's "idea," which differentiates the British from the Romans and from other conquerors but has, as it were, an intellectual rather than a spiritual reality.

The primary narrator views English history with reverence and sees in it a quasi-divine "spirit of the past," uniting "all the men of whom the nation is proud." Marlow considers the conquest of the earth "not a pretty thing" (p. 10), and he recognizes that before the Roman conquest the Britons too were "savages" (p. 9). Whereas the narrator sees in the national life a hallowed tradition at the root of England's ability to bear the light of civilization out to the rest of the world, Marlow seems uncomfortably aware that the idea is something closer to mere custom, a mental habit resulting from a series of more or less chance events that happens to have given the English a devotion to efficiency that other nations lack. Despite his inability to account for his own behavior from anything but an ethical standpoint, Marlow takes a somewhat more detached, sociological attitude toward the nation than the primary narrator does. We need the idea, Marlow suggests, because in this age without idols we need something to worship, something that can redeem our otherwise selfish and meaningless acts. Whereas the primary narrator is a willing participant in English history who unself-consciously records his observations on it, Marlow is an observer who wishes to take a skeptical, objective stance but whose scientific credentials are undermined by his evident emotional need to participate in the national myth. Just as Marlow will later feel himself unaccountably drawn toward Kurtz, in these opening pages of the story he already feels his objectivity to be compromised by too close an identification with his subject.

Marlow's partial submission to the primary narrator's providential account of English history corresponds to his general sense of the importance of accident or mere contingency in political affairs. His ethical stance toward the events of his story reflects his primary concern with the unique individual rather than with the broader movements of history. He remarks near the end of his story: "Destiny. My destiny! Droll thing life is—that mysterious arrangement of merciless logic for a futile purpose" (p. 69). Marlow's attitude toward the stories he tells is a bemused fatalism that leads him to place enormous stress on the notion of character in his analysis of events. As an alternative to Kurtzian idealism about human nature, Marlow continually speaks of the importance of "character," "innate strength," and internal "restraint." He respects the accountant's "starched collars and got-up shirt-fronts" as "achievements of character" that seem to enable the accountant to maintain not only his appearance but also his integrity "in the great demoralisation of the land" (p. 21). Marlow is satisfied that his English listeners possess character and restraint, which they have learned as members of a developed civil society: "What saves us is efficiency—the devotion to efficiency." He is less certain, however, about which other groups possess the virtues necessary to the development of civilization. The lack of "external checks" (p. 25) in Africa puts a high premium on internal "restraint." Marlow is disturbed by Kurtz's lack of "restraint" and is amazed to find the hired cannibals aboard his steamboat possessed of it, which they show by not eating their white masters although they outnumber them thirty to five (pp. 42–43). Even the hollow Manager, whom Marlow despises, "would wish to preserve appearances. That was his restraint" (p. 43).

Marlow finds the qualities of character and restraint to be unevenly distributed among individuals, probably at birth ("innate"). Despite his reputation among modern critics as a racist, however, he does not find any particular ethnic group to have a monopoly on "restraint" (although the English do well in his account). In fact, he frequently notes the common humanity of Africans and Europeans. He draws attention to the potentially disturbing thought that "savage" customs originate in the same impulses as "civilized" ones, for example in his reference to "the tremor of far-off drums, sinking, swelling, a tremor vast, faint; a sound weird, appealing, suggestive, and wild—and perhaps with as profound a meaning as the sound of bells in a Christian country" (p. 23). Marlow, like many a Victorian anthropologist (as Stocking has shown), has an abiding faith in the unity of human nature despite the diversity of its manifestations. In this respect he resembles other of Conrad's English heroes whose idealism blinds them to the effects of cultural differences, such as Jim in *Lord Jim* and Charles Gould in *Nostromo*. Marlow's experiences in the Congo temper this faith, but it never leaves him entirely, and, indeed, it seems to motivate his attachment to Kurtz.

Just as Marlow's own musings on the savagery of pre-Roman Britain seem to call into question the fairly conventional nationalism and historical optimism of the primary narrator, Marlow's account of his "choice of nightmares" in the Congo will itself problematize his more skeptical account of English culture. For, as it turns out, even the devotion to efficiency and the other saving graces of civilized life nearly desert Marlow in the Congo. Strangely enough, it is his very faith in civilization, progress, and especially the English way of doing things that seems to lead him to make what he himself calls his "strange" and "unforeseen" (p. 67) choice of nightmares. It is in the story's second installment that Marlow becomes irrationally attached to Kurtz, the man whose "moral ideas" have already made him curious.

Appeals to his nationality mark every stage of Marlow's recruitment to the "gang of virtue." Overhearing a conversation between the Manager and his uncle about Kurtz, Marlow learns of Kurtz's assistant, the "English half-caste clerk," whose "great prudence and pluck" in carrying out his mission Marlow admires, while the Manager and his uncle consider him a "scoundrel" (p. 34). Marlow soon heads up the river with several of the Company's pilgrims. As he gets closer to Kurtz, Marlow, "travelling in the night of first ages" (p. 37), contemplates his distant kinship with the savages who dance on the shore. He meets what he takes to be his first sign of a nearer kinsman when he comes across a hut recently inhabited by a white man, the Russian harlequin—known to the manager only as a trader who has intruded on the Company's protected interests. Marlow discovers the harlequin's copy of

> *An Inquiry into some Points of Seamanship* by a man Towser, Towson—some such name—Master in His Majesty's Navy.... The simple old sailor with his talk of chains and purchases made me forget the jungle and the pilgrims in a delicious sensation of having come upon something unmistakably real. (p. 39)

Marlow experiences his encounter with the book by the English sailor as a brief contact with the "real" in the midst of his dreamlike voyage. When he has to leave off reading the book, Marlow assures his listeners, it "was like tearing myself away from the shelter of an old and solid friendship" (p. 40). The original owner's fascination with the *Inquiry* impresses Marlow, especially when he mistakes the marginal notations in Russian for cipher.[43] He considers the use of cipher "an extravagant mystery" and comments aloud that the book's owner "must be English." The Manager responds to this observation with hostility: "It will not save him from getting into trouble if he is not careful" (p. 40). Marlow reports to his listeners: "I observed with assumed innocence that no man was safe from trouble in this world."

Marlow feels a bond of national solidarity with the imagined English trader, who has thwarted Belgian protectionism and devoted himself to studying the work of an English sailor. The shared text of Towser or Towson helps to cement the gang of virtue's claims on Kurtz's new recruit. It is at this point in the story that Marlow breaks off his narrative to recount the most spectacular appeal to nationality in Kurtz's own claim to kinship with him and his assurance that "his sympathies were in the right place." Marlow apparently treats Kurtz's appeal to his sympathies with some irony of his own, prefacing it with the remark "as he was good enough to say himself"—which seems to distance Marlow from the content of Kurtz's claim, even though the remainder of the story will show Marlow himself developing unexpected sympathies for Kurtz.

After relating Kurtz's appeals to their shared English "sympathies," Marlow describes the final stretch of the journey to the inner station. When he arrives and finally meets the Russian harlequin, that other admirer of Mr. Kurtz, the question of nationality arises again almost immediately: "The harlequin on the bank turned his little pug-nose up to me. 'You English?' he asked all smiles. 'Are you?' I shouted from the wheel. The smiles vanished and he shook his head as if sorry for my disappointment" (p. 53). The harlequin immediately takes to Marlow, just as he admires all things English. Marlow and the harlequin seal their friendship by sharing some of Marlow's "excellent English tobacco," for which the Russian thanks him: "Now, that's brotherly. Smoke! Where's a sailor that does not smoke" (p. 54).[44] This act, mirroring the frequent sharing of tobacco on board the *Nellie* on the Thames, seems to complete Marlow's induction into the "gang of virtue." He has unwittingly become, at least in the eyes of the European pilgrims, "a partisan of methods for which the time was not ripe." "Ah," Marlow comments, "but it was something to have at least a choice of nightmares" (p. 62).

Marlow never offers an adequate account of his reasons for remaining loyal to Kurtz, for what he calls his "choice of nightmares" in the story's final installment. His reasons remain unclear to him until the end, but it seems that, after the struggle between his disgust at Kurtz's barbarism and his hatred for the Company's hypocrisy, the appeals to national sympathy and solidarity made by the harlequin and Kurtz in large part determine his choice. By the time he has arrived at Kurtz's station Marlow has almost inadvertently cast his lot with the gang of virtue. He tells the Russian harlequin that "as it happens, I am Mr. Kurtz's friend—in a way" (p. 62), and when the harlequin appeals to him as a "brother seaman" to protect Mr. Kurtz (just before disappearing into the wilderness with one final handful of "good English tobacco" [p. 63]), Marlow makes the promise that "Mr. Kurtz's reputation is safe with me" (p. 62). Later on, when Kurtz's Intended again appeals to Marlow's love for Kurtz, she says to him: "You were his friend. . . . His friend" (p. 73). Although he hesitates, Marlow accepts the designation. Yet why Marlow pronounces himself Kurtz's friend remains obscure, and the lie he tells the Intended about Kurtz's final words has become a crux of Conrad criticism. Marlow offers a quasi-sociological explanation of the lie, claiming that to reveal Kurtz's words ("the horror! the horror!") "would have been too dark—too dark altogether" (p. 76). While Marlow's general concern for the workings of civilization certainly explains this decision in part, his loyalty to Kurtz's memory seems also to result from his sense of their kinship. Marlow lies because he has allowed the sentiments of "brotherhood" and "friendship" to obscure his dedication to the truth: his sympathy for Kurtz and for the Intended blinds him. Conrad, in rejecting the social-democratic ideal of fraternity, observed in the letter to Cunninghame Graham that "there is already as much fraternity as there can be—and that's very little and that very little is no good." In Marlow's lie to the Intended, Conrad shows how the dream of fraternity can stand in the way of justice and truth. Kurtz and the harlequin have succeeded in their appeal to Marlow's "sympathies" as an Englishman. Without his recognizing it, they have interpellated him—"brother seaman"—and made him their own.

There is, then, one force that molds character and that Marlow seems unable to analyze to his own satisfaction. In "Youth" he wonders aloud what made a crew of apparently undisciplined English sailors obey him, a twenty-year-old second mate, when they knew that the ship they were trying to save was doomed to sink (help was nearby, so the sailors' lives did not depend on their success). Marlow denies that a sense of duty or a desire for glory or financial reward could have driven them:

> No; it was something in [the English sailors], something inborn and subtle and everlasting. I don't say positively that the crew of a French or German merchantman wouldn't have done it, but I doubt whether it would have been done in the same way. There was a completeness in it, something solid like a principle, and masterful like an instinct—a disclosure of something secret—of that hidden something, that gift of good or evil that makes racial difference, that shapes the fate of nations. ("Youth," p. 29)

The sailors' very Englishness, a force beyond their understanding or control, makes them act nobly in an emergency. Yet here Marlow's belief in the existence of a "hidden something" does not amount to any sort of racial theory of history. The uneven distribution of character appears to him as an inexplicable secret, and it just so happens that the English have more of it than other people. Marlow's pride in his Englishness does not lead him to pronounce race a "key to history";[45] even he feels threatened by the biological definition of national character when the Company Doctor tries to apply it scientifically to Marlow himself.

Marlow has proven unable to find a middle way between the idealistic theories of human nature espoused by Kurtz and the racism of the Company Doctor. He cannot account for the logic of the "hidden something" that has shaped his character and made him susceptible to the appeals of the gang of virtue. Conrad himself, in the 1919 author's note to his autobiographical *A Personal Record* (1912), refers to a force that seems to have molded his "character" and that is superficially similar to Marlow's "hidden something":

> The impression of my having exercised a choice between the two languages, French and English, both foreign to me, has got abroad somehow. That impression is erroneous. . . .
>
> . . . .
>
> I have a strange and overpowering feeling that [English] had always been an inherent part of myself. English was for me neither a matter of choice nor adoption. . . . it was I who was adopted by the genius of the language, which directly I came out of the stammering stage made me its own so completely that its very idioms I truly believe had a direct action on my temperament and fashioned my still plastic character.[46]

Marlow attributes the English sailors' uniqueness to an innate racial difference,[47] relatively untouched by cultural and educational forces, whereas Conrad claims that, despite his Polish birth and ancestry, the English language, a product of English history and culture, has decisively influenced the development of his character. Conrad's creation of Marlow seems to result largely from his desire to portray his own life experiences through the filter of an English version of himself.[48] Most of Marlow's experiences originate in Conrad's biography, but Marlow's Englishness marks him off from his Polish-born creator. Thus, the Marlow stories investigate the question of the transferability of cultural values and assumptions. Marlow, in his remarks about the "hidden something," identifies nationality closely with race and therefore puts an unbridgeable gap between each nation and her neighbors; Conrad implies that nationality, while it determines character and is beyond the conscious control of the individual, can be acquired, and it is thus primarily a matter of upbringing—nurture rather than nature.

The distinction between the cultural and the biological explanations of character corresponds to a broader distinction between two types of explanation of the motivations of an individual's behavior. In the quotation from *A Personal Record* Conrad expresses the subjective sense that he cannot imagine himself as he was before the English language influenced his character. He has a "strange and overpowering feeling" that English has always been a part of him, although it clearly has not objectively always been so: there was a time, "the stammering stage," before he knew English. It is only in retrospect, from his own perspective as a fully formed subject, that his development as an adoptive Englishman seems to have made English "an inherent part" of himself. This retrospective sense of the necessity of character—that is, the sense that his character has been formed almost automatically and without any conscious choice on his part—resembles Marlow's own sense in *Heart of Darkness* that he could not have chosen to act differently than he did in Africa. It is the sort of illusion that makes the forces by which culture shapes the individual inexplicable to that individual in his or her own ethical terms. The individual, whose character has been formed by the contingencies of birth and upbringing, senses that despite the conscious workings of the mind, some greater forces have shaped his or her destiny.

The nature of this necessity cannot be generalized as a universal, sociological law. The almost mechanistic claim that all people of a given nationality will necessarily act in a similar way in given circumstances coarsens the sense of retrospective necessity felt by the individual subject who attempts to explain his or her own actions with attention to the complex interpenetration between consciousness and circumstance. As an observer, Marlow blithely asserts the existence of a "hidden something" that motivates the sailors, but when the Company Doctor tries to make a similar claim about Marlow—that his nationality has determined his experience in a way beyond his control—he objects. He turns to the mode of autobiographical storytelling that allows him to assert his status as a unique individual, not simply a representative of a given type: "I hastened to assure him I was not in the least typical" (p. 15).[49] Conrad gives the reader a reason to doubt Marlow's claim, and the tension between Marlow's own account of his behavior and the possible deterministic reading of it suggested by the Doctor is a crucial element in the novel's irony.

The story's narrative method, which has made it a classic of English modernism, emphasizes Marlow's location within a culturally specific set of assumptions that he cannot escape. Marlow and his four English listeners cannot say clearly what it is about Marlow's story that has caused their unease, but they feel their optimistic outlook on English civilization to be threatened. Incapable of explaining his actions when confronted with the non-English in Africa, Marlow tells his story to four fellow Englishmen, and although telling his story seems to him the best way to lay the soul of Kurtz to rest, the storytelling does not result in a neat conclusion or solution. By making Marlow so incapable of explaining his own attachment to Kurtz, Conrad suggests that the liberal English nation-state represented by Marlow and his listeners faces a crisis it cannot comprehend. Its values—humanity, decency, justice, efficiency, liberty, and devotion to ideals—are culturally specific and on the verge of being outmoded. Since they depend so completely on a particular English character, which is the product of historical accident (or good luck), they are incapable of being exported to the rest of the world. When the devotees of an English-style liberalism attempt to apply it to places and peoples unsuited by character to liberal self-government, the result is either a fanatical idealism tinged with egalitarianism (à la Kurtz) that tears down all institutions, or a bureaucratic and hypocritical nightmare (like the Company's) in which the strongest take advantage of the weakest while cloaking their motives in the forms of law and liberalism.

The difficulty is that even the best-willed imperialists seem condemned to apply their own ethnocentric standards to the societies they encounter, and Conrad seems to find little reason to trust that even the most noble sounding of these standards—"humanity, decency and justice"—can really be applied impartially except, perhaps, within the context of a nation-state as fortunate as Conrad seems to believe England has been in the history of its constitutional arrangements and the development of its civil society. Even among this happy breed of men it may be that the ideals of neutral justice, rule of law, and universal standards of right conduct are little more than the totems of a particularly successful cult whose time is running out. At any rate, Conrad would like to believe that he, a stateless Pole, has successfully become an Englishman, but in *Heart of Darkness* he expresses a profound skepticism about whether Africans—or even Belgians and Frenchmen—can do the same. For this reason, if for no other, Conrad's "national idea" has no future.

NOTES

1. Joseph Conrad, "Youth," in *"Youth" and Two Other Stories* (New York: Doubleday, Page, 1924), p. 3.

2. *Heart of Darkness: An Authoritative Text, Backgrounds and Sources, Criticism, Third Edition*, ed. Robert Kimbrough (New York: W. W. Norton, 1988), pp. 16, 12. All further references are to this edition.

3. Achebe, "An Image of Africa," *Massachusetts Review*, 18 (1977), 788; and Sarvan, "Racism and the *Heart of Darkness*," *International Fiction Review*, 7 (1980), 8.

4. See *Culture and Imperialism* (New York: Alfred A. Knopf, 1993), pp. 25, 69. In this work Said shows his own almost Conradian ambivalence about Conrad's attitudes toward empire.

5. *The Political Novels of Joseph Conrad: A Critical Study* (Chicago: Univ. of Chicago Press, 1963), p. 154. Hay defends her earlier interpretation, with more attention to the ambivalence of Marlow's attitude, in a recent article: "Rattling Talkers and Silent Sooth-Sayers: The Race for *Heart of Darkness*," *Conradiana*, 24 (1992), 167–78. In her short but important essay "Conrad and England" Benita Parry, after briefly tracing the multiple contradictions in Conrad's attitude toward his adoptive country, still oversimplifies the case by making an untenable distinction between Conrad's devotion to the nation as an ideal and what she considers his critical attitude toward the real, historical England: "It is true that Conrad's fictions do affirm patriotism as the noblest sentiment, racial solidarity as the ultimate loyalty, and a sense of national identity as essential to right conduct, but these are not injunctions to submit to the historically constituted British nation. Thus the panegyrics to Home are not to England but to a mystically conceived ideal, to the idea of a national culture as a spiritual realm, a moral republic" (Benita Parry, "Conrad and England," in *Patriotism: The Making and Unmaking of British National Identity. Volume III: National Fictions*, ed. Raphael Samuel [London: Routledge, 1989], p. 196). Hunt Hawkins gave an interesting talk on "Conrad's Idea of Englishness" at the Joseph Conrad Society meeting in Washington, D.C., 29 December 1996, emphasizing in particular Conrad's admiration for things English.

6. See Homi K. Bhabha, *The Location of Culture* (London: Routledge, 1994), pp. 85–92.

7. See *Heart of Darkness*, p. 10; Conrad, letter to Aniela Zagórska, 25 December 1899, in *The Collected Letters of Joseph Conrad*, ed. Frederick R. Karl and Laurence Davies, 5 vols. to date (Cambridge: Cambridge Univ. Press, 1983–), II, 230; Conrad, "An Observer in Malaya" (1898), rpt. in *Joseph Conrad on Fiction*, ed. Walter F. Wright (Lincoln: Univ. of Nebraska Press, 1964), p. 51; and Conrad, letter to Roger Casement, 21 December 1903, in *Collected Letters*, III, 96.

8. See Edmund Burke, *Reflections on the Revolution in France*, ed. J.G.A. Pocock (Indianapolis: Hackett Publishing, 1987), p. 28.

9. See Tratner, *Modernism and Mass Politics: Joyce, Woolf, Eliot, Yeats* (Stanford: Stanford Univ. Press, 1995); and Levenson, *Modernism and the Fate of Individuality: Character and Novelistic Form from Conrad to Woolf* (Cambridge: Cambridge Univ. Press, 1991).

10. Ian Watt has described the contradiction in the story's attitude toward "the Victorian ethic" in his section "Ideological Perspectives: Kurtz and the Fate of Victorian Progress," in his *Conrad in the Nineteenth Century* (Berkeley and Los Angeles: Univ. of California Press, 1979), pp. 147–68.

11. I draw the concept of "interpellation" from Louis Althusser, "Ideology and Ideological State Apparatuses (Notes towards an Investigation)," in his *Lenin and Philosophy and Other Essays*, trans. Ben Brewster (New York: Monthly Review Press, 1971), pp. 127–68; and Judith Butler, *Bodies that Matter: On the Discursive Limits of "Sex"* (New York: Routledge, 1993). I use the term in a very concrete sense, such as Althusser recognized when he gave the example of "that very precise operation which I have called *interpellation* or hailing, and which can be imagined along the lines of the most commonplace everyday police (or other) hailing: 'Hey, you there!'" ("Ideology," p. 174).

12. Joseph Conrad, *Lord Jim*, ed. Thomas Moser (New York: W. W. Norton, 1968), p. 27.

13. See Georg Lukács, *The Theory of the Novel: A Historico-Philosophical Essay on the Forms of Great Epic Literature*, trans. Anna Bostock (Cambridge, Mass.: M.I.T. Press, 1971).

14. Heracleitus, fragment 119 DK, quoted in Bernard Williams, *Shame and Necessity* (Berkeley and Los Angeles: Univ. of California Press, 1993), p. 136.

15. On the spoken story and the written novel, see Walter Benjamin, "The Storyteller: Reflections on the Works of Nikolai Leskov," in his *Illuminations*, ed. Hannah Arendt, trans. Harry Zohn (New York: Schocken, 1969), pp. 83–110; and Hannah Arendt, *The Human Condition* (Chicago: Univ. of Chicago Press, 1958).

16. See Said's chapter "Two Visions in *Heart of Darkness*," in *Culture and Imperialism*, pp. 19–31. On the historical context of this development, see H. Stuart Hughes, *Consciousness and Society: The Reorientation of European Social Thought, 1890–1930*, rev. ed. (New York: Vintage, 1977).

17. *Conrad's Politics: Community and Anarchy in the Fiction of Joseph Conrad* (Baltimore: Johns Hopkins Press, 1967), p. 10. Fleishman sees in Conrad a critic not only of individualism but of the related philosophies of liberalism in politics and utilitarianism in ethics.

18. Conrad, letter to George T. Keating, 14 December 1922, in *The Portable Conrad*, ed. Morton Dauwen Zabel (New York: Penguin Books, 1976), pp. 752–53. Conrad's few recorded comments on British formal politics suggest that despite his scorn for the more socialistic and democratic of the Liberal party's policies, he admired some traditional Liberal politicians—such as John Morley, the disciple of John Stuart Mill and biographer

of Gladstone who also wrote two books on Burke—and disliked certain aspects of the Conservatives' handling of the Boer War. See the following letters and the corresponding notes: to Spiridion Kliszczewski, 13 October 1885, in *Collected Letters*, I, 12; and to John Galsworthy, 15 November 1909, 27 November 1909, and 5 August 1910, in *Collected Letters*, IV, 288–90, 292, and 353–54.

19. On the relevance of the development of political liberalism to the earlier history of the novel, see Catherine Gallagher, *The Industrial Reformation of English Fiction: Social Discourse and Narrative Form, 1832–1867* (Chicago: Univ. of Chicago Press, 1985).

20. Conrad, letter to R. B. Cunninghame Graham, 8 February 1899, in *Collected Letters*, II, 157–58. Part of the letter was written in French (all translations are my own). Most critics see in this letter primarily a reactionary conservatism. In *Political Novels* Hay attempts to defend Conrad from this label, but she considers his nationalism primarily from a biographical rather than a theoretical point of view (see pp. 19–24). Parry describes the letter as reflecting "a conservatism wholly un-English" (p. 190), whereas I see in it a conservative liberalism quite English indeed. Fleishman suggests that the contradictions inherent in his position simply "seem not to have occurred to Conrad" and leaves it at that (p. 29). Watt quotes the letter as evidence for Conrad's view of solidarity but does not analyze the importance of the specifically national content of this solidarity (see p. 327). In his early work *Joseph Conrad and the Fiction of Autobiography* (Cambridge, Mass.: Harvard Univ. Press, 1966) Edward W. Said reprints this letter in full (pp. 201–3) and calls it "one of [Conrad's] most impressive" (p. 137), but he refers to Conrad's "idée nationale" as simply a "sub-rational sentiment" (p. 138) and equates it entirely with Marlow's "idea" that redeems imperialism. For a full annotation of the letter, see *Joseph Conrad's Letters to R. B. Cunninghame Graham*, ed. C. T. Watts (Cambridge: Cambridge Univ. Press, 1969), pp. 116–22, 204–5.

21. "The national idea," "an idea without a future."

22. "Egoism saves everything—absolutely everything—all that we love and all that we hate."

23. "The democratic idea is a very beautiful phantom"; "the shades of an eloquence that is dead precisely because it has no body."

24. See Fleishman, pp. 51–77.

25. Quoted in Kimbrough, p. 142. The most evident political theme of *Heart of Darkness* is, of course, the utter failure of the Congo Free State to live up to this propaganda. Conrad's loss of faith in the liberal idea of the nation resulted in part from this failure.

26. See Mill, *Considerations of Representative Government*, ed. Currin V. Shields (Indianapolis: Bobbs-Merrill, 1958), especially the final chapter, "Of the Government of Dependencies by a Free State," pp. 249–70.

27. "Man is a wicked animal. His wickedness must be organized."

28. These are all words associated with the liberals' inheritance from the eighteenth-century Whigs. See Stefan Collini, *Public Moralists: Political Thought and Intellectual Life in Britain, 1850–1930* (Oxford: Clarendon Press, 1991).

29. See *Victorian Anthropology* (New York: Free Press, 1987). See also J. W. Burrow, *Evolution and Society: A Study in Victorian Social Theory* (Cambridge: Cambridge Univ. Press, 1968).

30. See Hannah Arendt, *The Origins of Totalitarianism*, new ed. (New York: Harcourt Brace and World, 1966), p. 275; and E. J. Hobsbawm, *Nations and Nationalism since 1780: Programme, Myth, Reality* (Cambridge: Cambridge Univ. Press, 1990), p. 102.

31. Charles Adderley, quoted in Walter E. Houghton, *The Victorian Frame of Mind, 1830–1870* (New Haven: Yale Univ. Press, 1957), p. 47.

32. Conrad, letter to Aniela Zagórska, 25 December 1899, in *Collected Letters*, II, 230 (also quoted in Parry, p. 194). In *Political Novels* Hay reads *Heart of Darkness* as a veiled criticism of contemporary government policy in Africa, but actually Conrad vacillated on the issue of the war. Conrad goes on in this letter to attribute the Boers' essentially despotic character to their Dutch ancestry and to blame the war on German influence in Africa. For fuller accounts of his attitudes toward the war, see Hay, *Political Novels*, pp. 117–28; and Fleishman, pp. 129–31.

33. Karl Pearson, *National Life from the Standpoint of Science: An Address Delivered at Newcastle, November 19, 1900* (London: A. and C. Black, 1901), pp. 27–28. Pearson argued that the essential struggle for the survival of the fittest was among nations, not individuals.

34. Thomas H. Huxley, *Evolution and Ethics and Other Essays* (New York: D. Appleton, 1898), p. 37.

35. Jean-Jacques Rousseau, *Émile, or On Education*, ed. and trans. Allan Bloom (New York: Basic Books, 1979), p. 67.

36. In his letter to Cunninghame Graham, Conrad uses a similar phrase to describe the position of the extreme anarchists: "Je souhaite l'extermination générale" ("I hope for general extermination"). Conrad respects this statement because it is just, or perhaps simply accurate ("juste"), and straightforward ("clair"). His respect for the extreme anarchist resembles Marlow's for Kurtz: "He had summed up—he had judged" (*Heart of Darkness*, p. 69).

37. Watt quotes Camus on the need "in order to be a man, to refuse to be a God" (Watt, p. 168).

38. See Stocking, pp. 66–67. The polygenetic tradition continued to influence post-Darwinian racists such as Karl Pearson.

39. See Monygham's conversation with Mrs. Gould in chapter 11 of part three of Joseph Conrad, *Nostromo: A Tale of the Seaboard*, ed. Keith Carabine (New York: Oxford Univ. Press, 1984), p. 511.

40. The three are "Youth," *Heart of Darkness*, and *Lord Jim*. *Lord Jim* turned out to be too long, so Conrad replaced it with "The End of the Tether" (see Hay, *Political Novels*, p. 128).

41. The characters aboard Marlow's ship *Judea* in "Youth" are "Liverpool hard cases" (p. 25), whereas the crew on the real ship *Palestine*, on which Conrad based the *Judea*, included four non-Britons. The real-life crew of the *Narcissus* are similarly anglicized and fictionalized in *The Nigger of the "Narcissus"* (1897). See John Batchelor, *The Life of Joseph Conrad: A Critical Biography* (Oxford: Blackwell, 1994), pp. 34–36; and Watt, p. 92.

42. Joseph Conrad, *The Nigger of the "Narcissus": A Tale of the Sea*, ed. Jacques Berthoud (New York: Oxford Univ. Press, 1984), p. 163.

43. This is a mistake that Conrad himself would never have made and that again emphasizes Marlow's Englishness in contrast with Conrad's Polish origin.

44. The counterpart of the Russian harlequin in Francis Ford Coppola's "Apocalypse Now," an American journalist played by Dennis Hopper, greets Willard (the film's Marlow) by shouting out to him "I'm an American" and then snagging a pack of Marlboros.

45. See Arendt, *The Origins of Totalitarianism*: "For an ideology differs from a simple opinion in that it claims to possess either the key to history, or the solution for all the 'riddles of the universe,' or the intimate knowledge of the hidden universal laws which are supposed to rule nature and man" (p. 159).

46. Joseph Conrad, "Author's Note" (1919) to *A Personal Record*, in *"The Mirror of the Sea" and "A Personal Record,"* ed. Zdzislaw Najder (New York: Oxford Univ. Press, 1988), pp. iii, v.

47. It is important to note here that the idea of "race" itself was undergoing change in the 1890s. What had been a general term including both cultural and biological components of group membership increasingly took on, in the wake of Darwinism, its modern, primarily biological overtones. See Stocking.

48. See Batchelor: "As far as one can judge, Marlow seems to be *the kind of Englishman whom Conrad would have liked to have been*" (p. 34). Perhaps it would be better to say, "a kind of Englishman that Conrad could imagine himself having been."

49. The primary narrator seems to shore up Marlow's assertion of uniqueness when he observes that Marlow "did not represent his class" (the class of seamen) (p. 9). For the argument of this paragraph, see also Arendt, *The Human Condition*, pp. 181–88; Williams, *Shame and Necessity*, pp. 136–40 and passim; Butler, *Bodies that Matter*, pp. 93–119; Althusser, "Ideology and Ideological State Apparatuses"; and Benjamin, "The Storyteller."

HANS ULRICH SEEBER

Surface as Suggestive Energy: Fascination and Voice in Conrad's "Heart of Darkness"

Conrad's verbal art of arranging suggestive images and words, incidents and characters cannot, although by no means entirely foggy and impenetrable, be rendered adequately by discursive paraphrase and analysis. The poverty of reduction is the inevitable result. Still, the dialogue with such a text is equally inevitable, and if it is to yield results, it is probably best to explore, with the help of relevant contexts, the semantic and aesthetic implications, including the contradictions, of keywords such as, for example, "fascination" and "voice." It is precisely that which I propose to do in my paper. In "Heart of Darkness" there is, in fact, a chain of fascinations linking Europeans and Africans, Marlow, Kurtz and the listeners, fictional and nonfictional, through the medium of voices and sounds. Despite his emphasis on "seeing" in his famous "Preface" (1897) to *The Nigger of the "Narcissus"* ("to make you *see*"), which is in itself ambivalent, since "see" obviously refers to both sensual and intellectual cognition, Conrad's art of making an "appeal through the senses" relies just as much on hearing and listening. In his comment on Henry James, Conrad emphasizes the need of the novelist to speak out heroically on the eve of ultimate destruction, "to interpret the ultimate experience of mankind in terms of his temperament":

> He is so much of a voice that, for him, silence is like death; and the postulate was, that there is a group alive, clustered on his

From *Joseph Conrad: East European, Polish and Worldwide*, edited by Wieslaw Krajka: 215–235.
© 1999 by Maria Curie–Sklodowska University, Lublin.

threshold to watch the last flicker of light on a black sky, to hear the last word uttered in the stilled workshop of the earth. It is safe to affirm that, if anybody, it will be the imaginative man who would be moved to speak on the eve of that day without to-morrow.... ("Henry James: An Appreciation," *NLL*, 14)

Novels like *Lord Jim*, *The Nigger of the "Narcissus,"* "Heart of Darkness" and *Nostromo* are narrative studies in fascination and vocal effects. As we ponder on the specific quality they convey, as we ponder on our own fascination in the reading of these texts, we might well start from the insight that Conrad presents us a communicative act, in which we are invited to share in the fascination of observers, participants and oral narrators who seem to be in the thrall of a charismatic or rather pseudo-charismatic protagonist. Now fascination cannot be explained in terms of moral abstractions. The text of "Heart of Darkness" thus contains, among many others, two major tensions and contradictions, the second of which I propose to explore in my paper. First, in verbal art written at the turn of the century, the poetics of fascination depends for its effect on speech which lacks the unquestioned authority it used to have in religion and elsewhere. Second, rhetorically and ideologically, Marlow never quite abandons the traditional moral framework of good vs evil, culture vs nature; yet the fascination his language tries so hard to express and to convey is an irrational, quasi-religious experience which operates beyond the domain of the moral and the rational scheme of interpretation prevalent in the culture of nineteenth-century England.

FASCINATION

Fascination seems to be one of those terms which have as yet eluded the attention of the critics. In everyday language it denotes an unusual degree of attention which we give, for whatever reason, to an object of our experience. The intensity of the experience may be such as to freeze the experiencing subject into immobility or to release an explosion of emotional rhetoric trying to speak the unspeakable, i.e. the sort of strained language typical of Marlow. The experience is profoundly contingent, since it seems impossible to account for the huge variety of preferences and tastes that one encounters. Why is one person fascinated by butterflies, another one by a map of Africa? In a modern democratic culture, with its striking dissolution of belief systems and values, interest and fascination, in a sense fashion and style, are pretty much the only factors left to produce new relevancies and distinctions.

The interaction between subject and object called fascination operates beyond the domain of good and evil. What is involved is not a moral, but an aesthetic and, particularly in the context of archaic culture, a religious experience. Romantic literature has always known this. The seductive power of a *femme fatale* is, very much like that of a work of art or of a political Messiah, not due to her being the agent of the devil, but to properties like beauty, sexual attraction, energy and language. Pre-modern cultures endow the object of fascinated observation, or even awe, with magical properties. The fetish or the idol gain power over us, in a sense overwhelm our faculties, because they partake of supernatural energies. The quality of the experience is not affected by the fact that gods can be good or evil. Faced with what R. Otto calls the invisible presence of *"Das Numinose"* (*fascinans*, the holy) the mind of the religious person is filled with a mixture of happiness and fear, attraction and repulsion. Being both immeasurably powerful and deeply mysterious, the *mysterium tremendum* of the divine informs true religious experience with profound ambivalence. For ancient man, fascination is linked to the experience of a supernatural power existing beyond the boundaries of the familiar and the normal in life. In a sense, this is true even today. It is only the strikingly unusual, be it a charismatic person, an artistic achievement or a natural occurrence which is capable of producing fascination proper.

One might deem it superfluous to salvage possibly outmoded forms of consciousness from the ashes of oblivion. However, at the turn of the century philosophers, linguists, anthropologists and historians of culture developed an intense interest in prehistoric forms of thought and experience of which Conrad was not unaware. When scientific positivism and European culture reached in a sense an unprecedented height, a deep epistemological and cultural uneasiness concerning language in particular made itself felt. If the scientific paradigm of positivism does no longer suffice to explain the mystery of life, if abstract language in particular more and more appears to be futile rhetoric unable to express the bewildering complexity of life, then a writer could not but take recourse to the language of sensory experience, of myth and of parody. This is precisely what Conrad does in *The Nigger of the "Narcissus"* and "Heart of Darkness." He exploits the suggestive power and semantic richness of modern and ancient images and symbols for the purpose of making an effective aesthetic appeal. As they blend, interact and cancel out each other, a host of suggestions is produced which cannot be adequately paraphrased. (On this complexity see, for example, Fothergill, Burden). However, it seems to me that the negotiation between prehistoric and modern culture, sometimes translated by the text into a clash between nature vs corrupt civilization, sometimes into a clash between the disciplines ("work") of cultured life and the unrestrained play of wild, instinctual life, demonstrates, despite the frequent racist stereotyping of the natives, the superiority of the vital, irrational, physical, "natural" dimension of life over culture and morality as a source of fascination. Whether Marlow's moral rationalization of his final experience of Kurtz is to be taken at face value is at least doubtful. One could argue that Marlow's moral interpretation of Kurtz's "The horror! The horror!" is an illusion necessary for the preservation of his self-respect, just as his lie concerning Kurtz's last cry is necessary to keep the Intended's self-respect intact. The question is, of course, undecidable.

In Conrad's text, fascination is the effect on us of three media: image, voice and charismatic power, all of which belong both to premodern and to modern consciousness, to the age of idols, fetishes and prophet speaking to us out of the wilderness just as much as to the age of operas, gramophones, films, electronic media and dictators. In a sense, then, Kurtz's relapse into atavism is accompanied, on the level of novelistic discourse, by a reversion to modes of communication which are simultaneously modern and archaic. Thus the word "fascination" itself is thoroughly modern, insofar as it refers, like "love," to the contingency of individual experience, and yet it also reminds us of its origins in the premodern, magical thinking of ancient man. In Latin the verb *fascinare* means "to bewitch," "to enchant." It is no coincidence, therefore, that the skeptical Marlow is paradoxically likened to an idol and Buddha and that, like God, he is speaking to his listeners out of the dark, his body remaining unseen. By simulating Marlow's oral narrative, the novelist wishes to accomplish the required effect of "magic suggestiveness" ("Preface" to *The Nigger of the "Narcissus"*) which is identified by R. Otto in his famous study *Das Heilige* . . . (Otto, 80) as a major artistic mode in the representation of *das Numinose*. *Das Numinose* defines the specific irrational feeling of religious awe and fear, which is most powerfully present when the artist presents a "mixture of terrible fearfulness and most sublime holiness."[1] True, Kurtz must be called a profane and sinister, in short a modern travesty of Otto's *das Numinose*, but there is enough of the *Energie* (27) of the *Fascinans* (42) left in him to attract Marlow. Furthermore, Marlow himself is fascinated by the suggestive, awe-inspiring and incomprehensible silence of the wilderness, which, pregnant with undecoded meanings and menacing power, reminds one of the silence and the mysterious power of the god of mysticism. Otto links the experience of *das Numinose* with representations of Buddha in Chinese art (86).

It seems to me that the representation of Kurtz's voice also incorporates or at least alludes to elements of Christian discourse. The "gift" (see Corinthians I: 12) of speech proves Kurtz to be a creature of God. However, since he uses this gift without true "charity" (13: 1) he merely produces sounds without meaning, somewhat in the manner of a "sounding brass" (13: 1), and becomes "nothing" (13: 2). Yet, by a modern revaluation of values the absence of truth or meaning does not prevent the sounds, which prove the presence of an exceptional energy, from becoming the focus of an intense fascination. Again, the ambivalence of Kurtz's voice is reflected in Biblical language. The voice of the charismatic person reminds one both of a bodiless "voice from heaven" (Mark 1: 13) and, with a new complexity of meaning, of "the voice of one crying in the wilderness" (1: 3), who is both a prophet and a lost soul. For unlike Jesus, who resisted the temptations of the devil in the wilderness (1: 3), Kurtz yields to them. In other words, Kurtz radiates the fascination of a fallen god, and Marlow, being equally modern, feels attracted to him somewhat in the manner the romantics were attracted by the energy of Milton's Satan.

Conrad dramatizes and conceptualizes the experience of fascination. The word itself appears at crucial points in the unfolding of the story. Marlow ends his analogy of the Romans venturing into the wilderness of untamed Britain, which foreshadows his own report, on a sombre note of sympathetic speculation:

> He has to live in the midst of the incomprehensible, which is also detestable. And it has a fascination, too, that goes to work upon him. The fascination of the abomination—you know, imagine the growing regrets, the longing to escape, the powerless disgust, the surrender, the hate."
> He paused. ("Heart of Darkness," *YS*, 50)

Pauses are rare in Marlow's speech, and they invariably indicate profound significance and profound emotional involvement on the part of the speaker. The civilized explorer is both attracted and repelled by the call of the wild. If the "abomination" were so utterly alien and incomprehensible, it could hardly exert such a fascination. In *psychological* terms, the traveller and artist in fact responds to what Freud would call the "repressed" in himself, which is immediately censored by conscience. Does Conrad vacillate between moral and psychological models of interpretation? Or is the need to explore the psychological truth of wilderness without (the "savages") and within (Marlow) contaminated by the artistic need to find an appropriate rhetorical and ideological medium of communication? If the latter is true, words like "abomination," "fiend-like," "devil," "darkness" and the like are merely used to reach the audience rather than to camouflage a psychological insight. *In terms of literary history* Conrad rewrites the romantic fascination for the energy of the satanic. *In terms of colonialist discourse* Conrad wavers between subversive fascination and traditional contempt for the natives, understanding appreciation and conventional stereotyping of the barbaric other as utterly alien and incomprehensible.

There is apparently no rhetorical substitute for the connotative power of language and images charged with traditional meanings. Since scientific discourses cannot be scrapped, this frequently leads to a highly suggestive coexistence of scientific and mythical meanings. As a young man and romantic dreamer, Marlow is charmed by maps of far-off countries, the Congo in particular. As artist and narrator, he interprets his fascination with the river Congo in the following manner: "And as I looked at the map of it in a shop-window, it fascinated me as a snake would a bird—a silly little bird" (52). As a grown-up person, he decides to let his early fascination determine the course of his life: "The snake had charmed me" (53). The most fascinating object he meets on his travels is, however, not wilderness in its purity, but a contorted, even pathological blending of wilderness and refined culture, Mr. Kurtz. If one reads, as one surely must, the word "snake" as a deliberate reference to Biblical language, Marlow's confession is a profoundly disconcerting and romantic one: he becomes attracted to evil itself. If one takes up the clue offered by the interpretive comparison, Marlow is simply the victim of a biological and psychological affinity, a human animal which in a sense cannot help being devoured by another one. In the latter case the source of the fascination is predominantly to be found in vital energy operating under the conditions of modern culture.

I shall now make an attempt to substantiate this claim by exploring the semantic layers which seem to be suggested by the text when one reads the term "voice" in the light of medical discourse (Miethe, Hermann-Röttgen), sociological theories of the charismatic person (Weber) and the contemporary critique of language (Mauthner). According to medical discourse, the voice is shaped by three factors: the body, the psyche and the culture in which the speaking individual happens to live. The semantics of this grid provided by medical discourse do not exhaust the meaning, let alone the procedures, of a near-poetic text like "Heart of Darkness." What I have to do, therefore, is to explore a complex suggestiveness which is engendered by the interaction of scientific and symbolic meanings.

A Voice! A Voice!

exclaims Marlow. Clearly the fascination Kurtz induces in him is focused upon Kurtz's voice. A voice cannot be reduced any further. It expresses the very individuality and the very temperament of a person. Yet, judging from the voice, Kurtz's individuality seems to be curiously limited. There is no attempt to specify the quality of his voice. We only learn that it is deep and strong. Thus Kurtz appears to be a "remarkable person," as witnessed by his remarkable effects on other persons, but the very quality which accounts for his individuality in particular, and its extraordinary effect on others is comparatively unspecific as far as the words of the text are concerned. If one assumes, as I do, that Conrad's novel fascinates the reader by a combination of charismatic person and charismatic text, the seeming contradiction indicated above makes sense. The charismatic person is essentially a type maintaining its identity best when viewed from a distance. Not surprisingly, we never get an inside view of the mind of Kurtz. It relies for his or her power over others on vocal and suggestive communication rather than the written word. The voice of the charismatic person is, like the voice of God, the law itself, but, unlike the voice of God, it is also the expression of his psychophysical identity. It is therefore extremely abstract and extremely individual at the same time. The voice expresses individuality and yet partakes of the universality of a social and psychological type. The "magic suggestiveness," required of the speech of the charismatic speaker, is not brought about by the precision of quasi-scientific or quasi-historical language. It presupposes a language which is indefinite and full of blank spaces, thus inviting the imaginative participation of the reader. Again, not surprisingly, there is no scene showing Marlow and Kurtz speaking to each other at length.

Before pursuing this point further, a brief look at the history of voice in novelistic discourse before Conrad is necessary. Unlike Bakhtin, for whom the term "voice" is a metaphoric substitute for "social heteroglossia" (Bakhtin, 263), i.e. the combination of socially determined styles to be found in a novel, I use the term "voice" in the strict semiotic and linguistic meaning of "vocal communication." In the history of English novel before Conrad the quality of vocal communication was never paid much attention, neither in theory, where the term is hardly ever used, nor in the fictional texts themselves simulating oral speech to characterize individuals and tellers of tales like Marlow. In order to acknowledge the act of speaking, Jane Austen usually confines herself to using the verbs "said," "replied" or "cried." The huge variety of meaningful tones or, as linguists say, "vocal stereotypes," was largely ignored as the individual's identity was supposed to unfold itself in his acts and the content of his speeches. However, Gothic novels, focusing on the spectacular delineation of passions, used a wider spectrum of verbal possibilities and generally the development towards psychological realism in Eliot and others meant that the representation of subjectivity implied giving greater attention to nuances of tone. Still, voice continued to play a subsidiary role in characterization and the separation of voice from content which we find in Conrad was unthinkable.

I suggest three possible reasons for the striking importance attributed to voice at the turn of the century. First of all, Nietzsche's critique of idealism and metaphysics and his praise of the body turned the assumptions of occidental philosophy upside down. Psychologists like Wilhelm Wundt regarded man as a psychophysical unity and medical researchers like Barth contributed classic studies of the physiology and pathology of the voice. Second, the recent invention of the gramophone separated enunciating body and voice and made the preservation of a huge variety of voices possible for future use and enjoyment. Joyce makes Bloom explicitly meditate on this phenomenon in the Hades chapter of *Ulysses*. In fact, in the year 1887, well before the publication of "Heart of Darkness," the *Deutsche Grammophon-Gesellschaft* offered the first gramophones for sale. Third, Immanuel Kant's critique of pure reason was transformed, in the course of the nineteenth century into a critique of language, the most influential work being F. Mauthner's *Beiträge zu einer Kritik der Sprache*.[2] For Mauthner the modern languages of culturally advanced societies are not neutral and effective tools necessary for human communication and cognition. On the contrary, they exert a "tyranny" (Mauthner, 1) over us, defining the range of our ideas. Language cannot be reduced to a function of logic and grammar. As an act and as a power (47), it has a suggestive energy like someone subjecting us to a "hypnosis" (43). This is particularly the case when words become, in the course of time, divorced from their roots in sensory experience and metaphor and acquire the status of empty discursive husks, of "dead word symbols" (66). Theology, philosophy, science and political theory are endlessly producing abstractions of this kind, words like "progress" and "evolution" (25), whose very emptiness gives room for endless speculations and associations for those users who have not lost their belief in them. According to Mauthner, the most striking symptom of the decadence of modern culture is the theatrical quality of its language (230). In his seminal work, cultural criticism thus becomes a criticism of language. The languages of modern culture are degenerate playthings (51), unable to express feelings or to enable real communication or to increase our knowledge. Instead, they produce endless misunderstandings (56).

The relevance of all this for the language of Kurtz and Marlow is obvious. Marlow dismisses Kurtz's political and humanitarian rhetoric as fundamentally false and obsolete. The official discourse of progressive philanthropic colonialism, endlessly repeated by the newspapers, is for him simply "rot" and "humbug" ("Heart of Darkness," *YS*, 59). Examples are highlighted for the sake of ironic distancing. If Kurtz still impresses Marlow, it is therefore not by virtue of the meanings transported, but by virtue of the suggestive power of something physical and psychological, i.e. the voice itself. The text seems to be completely or perhaps strategically silent on the question whether a physical, homoerotic attraction is implied. Whatever the answer to this question, the relationship between depth and surface becomes inverted. It is the vocal surface itself, the materiality of the sign, which causes an effect. It appears as if the deep structure of meaning were replaced or at least rivalled by effects emanating from the suggestive energy of the surface.

Mauthner does not quite envisage the radical possibility and logical consequences of his thought sketched here. Yet his description of the properties of literary language, which partly recovers the sensuous saturation of archaic language, to some extent explains Marlow's stylistic procedure. Words are essentially imprecise, particularly when they are positioned in a literary organization. Since they have blurred, moving edges (*flimmernd und zitternd*—Mauthner, 109) every recipient is expected to flesh out, with the help of memory and imagination, the suggestions of the text in his own way.

Conrad, like Mauthner, realizes that abstract terms such as "voice" offer a particularly wide range of interpretive possibilities, especially when rhetorical emphasis and context invite the reader to activate their semantic potential. I distinguish six meanings of the sign "voice" in Conrad's text, the first three of which are all related to its psychophysical properties:

(a) Kurtz's deep, ringing voice is emphatically *male*. The fact has causal and symbolic implications. Only a male and only an exceptionally big male— the text mentions seven feet—possesses the required size of the chest and of the vocal cords to do this. On the symbolic level, the huge male conforms to the notion of the romantic hero who is of course deconstructed by the ironic naming device.

(b) The second and less obvious cause of Kurtz's voice might be, very much like that of Wait in *The Nigger of the "Narcissus,"* the *pathological* state of his body, which again suggests connotations of psychological, ethical and cultural breakdown.

(c) What Marlow responds to is primarily not Kurtz's moral depravity or the poignancy of the protagonist's thwarted utopian ambitions, but the sheer presence of *energy*: "The volume of tone he emitted without effort, almost without the trouble of moving his lips, amazed me. A voice! a voice!" ("Heart of Darkness," *YS*, 135). "Though he could hardly stand, there was still plenty of vigour in his voice" (143). Since Kurtz's voice is the manifest sign of a vital force, the emptiness of his rhetoric is paradoxically able to enthrall the listener like magic. The fictional listeners are carried away by "a magic current of phrases" (118). For Marlow, Kurtz's voice, i.e. an aesthetic impression, is far more memorable than his actions. Representing a natural force, Kurtz is really a Darwinian and Nietzschean character, a superman and a Shavian life-force. In that respect he resembles another obsessive talker of contemporary literature, Shaw's Tanner in *Man and Superman*, who is also a would-be philanthropist and reformer, and whose rhetoric persuades not because it reveals the truth but because it epitomizes energy (Seeber).

(d) Numerous references to the powers of the dark, read in conjunction with Kurtz's utopian aspirations, suggest that Kurtz is interpreted by Marlow as a fallen God or a false prophet. The unique qualities of his character and his voice, far from having to be attributed to contingency, are in fact typical features of the charismatic personality.

As Levenson pointed out, Weber's analysis of charisma as a mode of rule is important for an understanding of "Heart of Darkness." Two points, however, need to be added to his reading. Weber is aware of the ambivalence of charisma, its roots in primitive consciousness and its persistence in modern guises, and he is also aware of the function of orality and voice in the practice of charismatic rule.

Weber's scientific, objective, value-free method of sociology does not distinguish between good and bad, god-like or devil-like charismatic leaders or a mixture of the two. Theologians apparently think otherwise, but from the point of view of Weber's sociology of rule, Kurtz is a charismatic person and also a parody of such a person. To have success with people, the charismatic leader needs personal qualities lifting him far above the domain of common humanity. He is, therefore, a god-like hero equipped with essentially magic powers. The charismatic leader is not subject to rules and rational procedures (not surprisingly the Manager complains of Kurtz's "unsound method"— "Heart of Darkness," YS, 137); his rule is, on the contrary, irrational, realized from moment to moment by creative actions. Not being bound to the rules of tradition and bureaucratic order, charismatic rule is decidedly revolutionary and unpredictable. Archaic warrior-leaders or religious prophets win recognition among devoted followers or disciples by spectacular deeds and words apparently inspired by supernatural powers. These words and deeds may get recorded in historical or holy texts to ensure an integrating effect on the followers of the charismatic person after his death. His chief weapon, however, is the power of the spoken word, the conjunction of body and voice, the *viva vox*, as Otto (80) calls it, which, as Jesus emphasizes, is not bound by written traditions.

The parallels between Weber's characterization of charismatic rule and Conrad's characterization of Kurtz are striking. Kurtz, assuming the role of a deity, establishes his charismatic leadership over the natives to such an extent that they even follow him when he, ill and emaciated, has to command them from a stretcher. The intriguing aspect of Weber's analysis, however, is his claim that charisma is also the essence of modern revolutionary leaders like Napoleon or the literary demagogue Kurt Eisner. Napoleon's rule is the "rule of genius" (Weber, 141) and it is precisely the demagogic genius (140) in the journalist and political speaker Kurtz who casts a spell over his audience. With uncanny premonition Conrad senses the conjunction between political and artistic genius in the ruthless political leaders of modernity. Kurtz, the prophet, succeeds in winning devoted "disciple(s)" ("Heart of Darkness," YS, 132) like the Russian, or devoted friends like Marlow. In each case it is the voice which does the trick. Kurtz is incapable of dialogue; he utters his judgements and commands in "splendid monologues" (132), forcing his environment—with the great exception of Marlow—to act as listeners. "He had the power to charm or to frighten rudimentary souls into an aggravated witch-dance in his honour" (119).

Clearly Marlow and Kurtz share many characteristics. Theirs is the charisma of artists who enthrall their audiences by the power of a voice which, divorced from the body, seems to act like an independent agent. Whereas Kurtz succumbs to the wilderness entirely, Marlow at least acknowledges the power of the call of the wild epitomized by the drums, realizing that culture is only a thin veneer concealing the reality of "primitive emotions" (147). The force of the latter forms a bond and a *chain of fascinations* between the exotic other, Marlow, Kurtz and the reader, the "grunting" natives and the "grunting" listeners on board the yacht.

(e) The fifth connotation associated with "voice" in "Heart of Darkness" concerns cultural and personal reduction. A person merely consisting of voice does no longer meet the criteria of a full human being: "The man presented himself as a voice" (113). "The voice was gone. What else had been there?" (150). Since the voice forms sounds deprived of real meaning, Marlow's memory is filled with an "immense jabber" (115), a bewildering pandemonium of various voices and noises. A voice divorced from the body and from meaning seems to float in the air like something unreal and absurd, ghostly and eerie. Thus voice is linked to the concepts of "unreality," "absurdity" and "dream" which are constantly used by Marlow to interpret his bewildering experience of colonialism's "fantastic invasion" of Africa (131). By metaphoric transfer Kurtz, "this eloquent phantom" (160) thus becomes a hollow man whose lack of inner, cultural substance causes the tremendous reverberation of his voice in an empty chest: "But the wilderness had found him out early, and had taken on him a terrible vengeance for the fantastic invasion. I think it had whispered to him things about himself which he did not know, things of which he had no conception till he took counsel with this great solitude—and the whisper had proved irresistibly fascinating. It echoed loudly within him because he was hollow at the core" (131).

Given all these contexts, "voice" suggests, in a highly complex fashion, contradictory meanings cancelling out each other: the voice of the hero, the voice of the dummy, the voice of the charismatic leader, the voice of absurdity and unreality. Divorced from the body, it is the meeting-point of modernity and primitive culture, the gramophone and God's or the prophet's *viva vox* (Otto, 79). Still, we must not forget that the reduction of language to voice discussed here is often viewed positively by contemporary poetics. Robert Frost, for example, emphatically bases his poetics of lyrical poetry on "sentence sounds" and "tones" (Scully, 50) which are not entirely subordinated to the meaning of the sentence. Mistrust of the emptiness of the written word, newspaper language in particular, is the critical impulse motivating Frost's preference for the vocal materiality of the sign. Artificial words without meaning, i.e. pure sounds form the materials of provocative sound poems by the Dadaist Hugo Ball as for example "Karawane" which can be made to represent something exclusively by the choice of intonation and stress. However, Conrad's prose text does not and cannot aim at such radicalism despite its use of pauses, elliptic sentence patterns and the like. It primarily invites us to explore its polyvalent, often contradictory meanings.

(f) This brings me to my sixth and last point. I believe one of the connotations suggested and teased out by the very blankness and repetitive weight of the term "voice" is related to the poetics of fascination. Conrad's well-known statements on his own art make this reading likely. The voice of Marlow, of Kurtz and of Conrad himself, are artistic voices speaking to us in a seemingly apocalyptic situation. Voice in this sense hints at the suggestive energy of the artist's utterance and the energy of the suggestive surface of visual and acoustic images. After all, the natives are largely a vocal presence who, as described by Darwin and Barth, express their elementary emotions of grief and anger through gestures and sounds ("howling" etc.).

My emphasis on *surface* needs to be justified. Throughout his narrative Marlow employs, when adopting the role of a cultural critic, the binary opposition reality vs appearance, depth vs surface. Like cultural critics of the nineteenth century, he appropriates a semantic opposition rooted deep in occidental epistemology for purposes of cultural criticism. Invariably the critics, analyzing modern man's specific alienation, diagnose a lack of inner substance and worth. So does Marlow. According to him, the irresponsible and greedy "pilgrims" chasing after the modern idol ivory in the Congo have "nothing inside but a little loose dirt" ("Heart of Darkness," *YS*, 81). Clothes hide no longer, as they do in Carlyle, the spirit of the absolute, but the "darkness" of "primitive emotions": "Kurtz discoursed. A voice! a voice! It rang deep to the very last. It survived his strength to hide in the magnificent *folds* (my emphasis) of eloquence the barren darkness of his heart" (147). However, since the truth of verbal signs and the reality of life can no longer be ascertained, all we seem to be left with is the suggestive energy of surfaces and styles. Conrad's text cannot be reduced to a mere attempt at rhetorical and opera-like effects, the sort of effect that is clearly evident on the occasion of Wait's first spectacular appearance in *The Nigger of the "Narcissus,"* when his ringing voice silences and enthralls the crowd of sailors, but it certainly inverts and thereby deconstructs the classical dichotomy of story and meaning, surface and depth. There is some truth in the anonymous narrator's claim that the suggestive surface of Marlow's story radiates meanings rather than encapsules them for the reader to uncover. This is indeed one of the characteristic tensions and paradoxes of Conrad's art: whereas Conrad, the moralist and cultural critic, denounces the surfaces of theatrical, operatic and rhetorical effects as hollow and empty lies, the artist Conrad very much relies on voice and image and rhetoric and the musical genre which makes the best use of them at the expense of meaning, i.e. the opera. Does the almost random production of incompatible meanings in "Heart of Darkness" "really" mean that both Marlow and we as readers are seduced by sounds and sights, by appearances and surfaces, including verbal surfaces, rather in the manner Baudrillard analyzes the effects of modern media? Such a thinking would certainly be compatible with Nietzsche's thinking in "Nietzsche contra Wagner":

> Oh those Greeks! they knew how to live. For that, it is necessary to stay bravely with the surface, the wrinkle, the skin, to worship appearance, to believe in forms, sounds, words, in the whole Olympus of appearance.... And are we not returning to this, we daring spirits who have climbed to the most elevated and dangerous top of contemporary thought and have looked around from there?[2]

Clearly, the relevance of Conrad's poetics of fascination is not confined to "Heart of Darkness." Whenever political demagogues like Donkin (*The Nigger of the "Narcissus"*), Gamacho, the Montero brothers (*Nostromo*) or other pseudo-charismatic characters as, for example, Wait (*The Nigger of the "Narcissus"*) appear on the scene, they seem to cast a magic spell over their audience by the sheer power of their voice and the theatrical quality of their gestures, actions and physical appearance. I have already pointed out the magic effect of Wait's voice on the crew. For the majority of the crowd listening to a speech by the revolutionary Pedrito Montero in *Nostromo*, the effect of fascination is created by merely watching the gestures of the speaker and listening to his voice, very much as if they were enjoying an operatic performance:

> What he began was a speech. He began it with the shouted word "Citizens!" which reached even those in the middle of the Plaza. Afterwards the greater part of the citizens remained *fascinated* [italics mine] by the orator's action alone, his tip-toeing, the arms flung above his head with the fists clenched, a hand laid flat upon the heart, the silver gleam of rolling eyes, the sweeping, pointing, embracing gestures, a hand laid familiarly on Gamacho's shoulder; ... (*N*, 389–90)

Conrad's caricature of political rhetoric emphasizes its histrionic, operatic quality. Rather than communicating "deep" thoughts and arguments, its "phrases" ("[T]he happiness of the people," "Sons of the country"—390), which are usually inaudible anyway, convey emotive suggestions, an attitude of passionate involvement, which is even better communicated by the political actor's quasi-theatrical performance. In this performance (primitive, animal-like) the quality of the voice plays a major role. It is chiefly due to its powerful presence that the trick of emotional persuasion is accomplished. Thus the "crowd" responds to "the howling voice of Gamacho" (391) by producing "vast, deep muttering" (391).

The discovery of atavism by medical science (Cesare Lombroso) at the turn of the century helps to undermine the stability of the classical binary opposition culture vs nature. According to a widely held notion shared, for example, by John Davidson and Aldous Huxley and fitting perfectly into their and Conrad's notion of cultural criticism, modern crowds in a sense behave like savages. Their unthinking devotion to a charismatic leader is, therefore, paralleled by the charismatic quality of Karain's rule over his followers in "Karain: A Memory." However, the reader of "Karain: A Memory" experiences the haunting voice in at least three functions and meanings. (1) The mere physical and vocal presence of Karain, the native chief, among his followers, induces in them acts of devotion and of respect. Karain has the effect of a magnet on the rest of the community. (2) As he tells his story of revenge, which ends in the catastrophe of Karain shooting his friend Matara rather than the Dutch lover of Matara's sister, the white listeners are enthralled both by the content and the oral style of Karain's tale, Karain's seemingly free-floating voice in particular. Similarly, the readers of Conrad's tale are meant to be enthralled by the artist's impressionistic evocation of the exotic setting. (3) The unbearable, haunting voice of Matara's ghost urging Karain to complete the revenge can only be neutralized by the intervention of a magic spell. After the death of Karain's sword-bearer and protector a spell is provided by Hollis, a white man, whose incantatory words and voice transform a ribbon and a jubilee sixpence representing Queen Victoria into a powerful amulet and fetish which restores Karain's self-confidence. What appears to be a mere hoax exploiting Karain's superstitions turns out to be an event which in fact calls into question the validity of binaries like West vs. East, rationalism vs. irrationalism, culture vs. nature, reality vs. fiction/illusion. After all the Western people have their ghosts, too, who suddenly return during the magic ritual performed by Hollis. Furthermore, the end of the text, raising the question of reality, contrasts Jackson's seeming preference for Karain's world with the narrator's insistence upon the superior status of "home," i.e. London. The question whether the sight of alienated urban crowds is more real than

Karain's strange experience remains undecided. It would appear, following the argument of this paper, that the suggestive energy of surfaces is potent in both cultures (one of which used to be subsumed under the category "nature" at the time), presumably because seeing images and hearing voices are also— explicitly so in the case of Karain—acts of believing. Such acts of believing turn mere surfaces, appearances or images, including verbal/vocal surfaces, into veritable truths, while lack of belief transforms truths into illusions. It seems to me correct to speak of the "real/illusory world" (Krajka, 255; see also Griem, 110 f.) created by Conrad. Due to belief, a deceptive imitation or fictional act acquires the status of a truth. The transgression of seemingly clear borderlines by Kurtz and by Hollis, and also by Marlow, the reader and, last but not least, the author himself, is a logical step implied in Conrad's epistemological, anthropological and aesthetic views. This step also reflects the nihilistic, Nietzschean episteme of the time. In *Götzen-Dämmerung* Nietzsche attacks the occidental notion and search for truth and pointedly gives one of his sections the title "Wie die 'wahre Welt' endlich zur Fabel wurde" (How the "true world" finally became a fiction) (Nietzsche, II, 963).

NOTES

1. "Mischung entsetzlicher Fürchterlichkeit und höchster Heiligkeit" (Otto, 81).

2. *"O diese Griechen! sie verstanden sich darauf, zu leben! dazu tut not, tapfer bei der Oberfläche, der Falte, der Haut stehnzubleiben, den Schein anzubeten, an Formen, an Töne, an Worte, an den ganzen Olymp des Scheins zu glauben! Diese Griechen waren oberflächlich,—aus Tiefe. . . . Und kommen wir nicht eben darauf zurück, wir Wagehalse des Geistes, die wir die höchste und gefährlichste Spitze des gegenwärtigen Gedankens erklettert und von da aus uns umgesehn haben"* (Nietzsche, II, 1061; quoted after Pfeiffer, 23).

WORKS CITED

Bakhtin M. M. *The Dialogic Imagination: Four Essays*, ed. Michael Holquist. Austin: U. of Texas P., 1985.

Barth Ernst. *Einführung in die Physiologie, Pathologie und Hygiene der menschlichen Stimme*. Leipzig: Thieme, 1911.

Burden Robert. *"Heart of Darkness": An Introduction to the Variety of Criticism*. Basingstoke: Macmillan, 1991.

Crystal David. *The Cambridge Encyclopedia of Language*. Cambridge: Cambridge U.P., 1987.

Ellis James. "Kurtz's Voice: The Intended as 'The Horror'," *English Literature in Transition* (1880–1920), 19 (1976), 105–10.

Fothergill Anthony. *"Heart of Darkness."* Milton Keynes: Open University Press, 1989.

Griem Julika. *Brüchiges Seemannsgarn: Mündlichkeit und Schriftlichkeit im Werk Joseph Conrads*. Tübingen: Narr, 1995; Script Oralia 81.

Krajka Wieslaw. "Making Magic as Cross-cultural Encounter: The Case of Conrad's 'Karain: A Memory'," *Conrad, James, and Other Relations*, eds. Keith Carabine and Owen Knowles with Paul Armstrong. Boulder–Lublin–New York: East European

Monographs–Maria Curie–Sklodowska University–Columbia U.P., 1998, 245–59; *Conrad: Eastern and Western Perspectives*, ed. Wieslaw Krajka, vol. 6.

Levenson Michael. "The Value of Fact in 'Heart of Darkness'," in Joseph Conrad. *"Heart of Darkness."* A Norton Critical Edition, ed. Robert Kimbrough, Third Edition. New York–London: Norton, 1988, 391–405.

Mauthner Fritz. *Beiträge zu einer Kritik der Sprache*. Erster Band: *Zur Sprache und zur Psychologie*. 2 Auflage. Stuttgart–Berlin: Cotta, 1906. Translations from this text are mine.

Miethe Erhard, Hermann-Röttgen Marion. *Wenn die Stimme nicht stimmt . . . Symptome, Ursachen, Therapie*. Stuttgart: Thieme, 1993.

Nietzsche Friedrich. *Werke in drei Bänden*, ed. Karl Schlechta. Darmstadt: Wissenschaftliche Buchgesellschaft, 1994.

Otto Rudolf. *Das Heilige: Über das Irrationale in der Idee des Göttlichen und sein Verhältnis zum Rationalen* (1917). München: Beck, 1987.

Pecora Vincent. "'Heart of Darkness' and the Phenomenology of Voice," *English Literary History*, 52: 4 (1985), 993–1015.

Pfeiffer K. Ludwig. "Suggestiveness or Interpretation: On the Vitality of Appearances," in *Reflecting Senses: Perception and Appearance in Literature, Culture and the Arts*, ed. Walter Pape and Frederick Burwick. Berlin–New York: Walter de Gruyter, 1995, 15–32.

Scully James, ed. *Modern Poets on Modern Poetry*. London: Fontana, 1971.

Seeber Hans Ulrich. "The 'Hero' Speaks. Energy and Verbal Power in Dramas of the Turn of the Century (Shaw, Synge)," in *Word and Action in Drama: Studies in Honour of Hans-Jürgen Diller on the Occasion of his 60th Birthday*, ed. Günter Ahrends et al. Trier: Wissenschaftlicher Verlag, 1994, 119–35.

Weber Max. *Wirtschaft und Gesellschaft: Grundriss der verstehenden Sociologie*. 5 Auflage. Tübingen: Mohr, 1976.

JAMES MORGAN

Harlequin in Hell:
Marlow and the Russian Sailor in
Conrad's Heart of Darkness

"Harlequin," C. G. Jung wrote, "gives me the creeps," due to the ambiguous nature of the archetype. As a result, Jung was unable to determine whether or not Harlequin as an archetype successfully passes through hell: "He is indeed the hero who must pass through the perils of Hades, but will he succeed? That is a question I cannot answer."[1] The Russian sailor in Conrad's *Heart of Darkness* is not the hero of the novella, but Marlow's identification of him as a harlequin who presents an "unsolvable problem" leaves readers similarly wondering what to make of the enigmatic character. He seems to reside like the "meaning" of one of Marlow's tales, "not inside like a kernel but outside, enveloping the tale which brought it out only as a glow brings out a haze."[2] Marlow's shifting responses to the Russian sailor and his own psychological imperatives, which cause him simultaneously to reveal and to conceal his identification with the Russian, create such an ambiguous haze compounded by our tendency as readers to interpret the Russian harlequin as a symbol rather than as an archetypal prototype who represents not a goal but a stage Marlow is only partially successful in passing through in his journey.

Marlow's initial responses to the Russian sailor, and those of many subsequent critics, derive from associations of Harlequin with the Commedia dell'Arte and the comic conventions of court jesters and fools. The Russian sailor immediately brings Harlequin to Marlow's mind by his "funny"

From *Conradiana* 33 (Spring 2001): 1–5. © 2001 by Texas Tech University Press.

appearance: the "parti-colored rags"[3] covering his clothing and his "extremely gay"[4] antic disposition. This association is reinforced by the sailor's mercurial disposition conveyed by rapid shifts in his speech and mood, "with smiles and frowns chasing each other over that open countenance like sunshine and shadow on a wind-swept plain."[5] Marlow is "seduced" into "something like admiration—like envy" for the sailor's obedience to the "absolutely pure, uncalculating, unpractical spirit of adventure" burning with a "modest and clear flame."[6] Surely Marlow shares the same spirit of adventure dating from the days he spent in childhood poring over the uncharted blank spaces in maps, "a white patch for a boy to dream gloriously over."[7] Nevertheless, Marlow distances himself from the Russian sailor by attributing to him a naive innocence prepared for rhetorically by the conventions of the fool: "I did not envy him his devotion to Kurtz, though. He had not meditated over it."[8] Attempting to disavow his own relationship to Kurtz, Marlow ridicules the Russian sailor as "Kurtz's last disciple."[9]

From Marlow's implicit identification with the Russian harlequin and explicit disavowal of that identification, critics have pursued wildly divergent analyses. On the one hand, John W. Canario sees the Russian as "a white aborigine" who through identification triggers in Marlow a "profound realization that aboriginal man possesses a capacity for humane behavior and a primitive sense of honor that makes him impervious to the greed that corrupts civilized Europeans" and is symbolized by Kurtz.[10] On the other hand, Jack Helder sees the Russian as a "traditional simpleton" whose "inability to understand his experience with Kurtz ... most distinguishes him from Marlow, and which finally renders him most sinister."[11] This harlequin belongs to the group of fools such as "hunchbacks, dwarves, etc." whose physical "deformity" reveals "the spiritual poverty manifested by the colonization movement, and by mankind in general" and thus "cannot be absolved from a strong measure of guilt for what happened to Kurtz . . . by his failure to represent any moral standard."[12] This "deformed simpleton devoid of moral sense" has "no mind at all" and "serves no useful function in the struggle of mankind against the forces of chaos."[13]

Reconciling such antithetical responses to the Russian sailor is complicated by Marlow's unreliability as narrator. Barry Stampfl points out that Marlow's expressed inability to understand the purpose of "a vast artificial hole" he "avoided" as he approached the Company's station, clearly a mass grave for the dying native workers, exposes the use of psychological repression to evade recognition of his complicity in the atrocities taking place.[14] Similarly Marlow asserts that his audience knows "I hate, detest, and can't bear a lie" because there is "a taint of death, a flavour of mortality in lies,"[15] but of course ends his tale by revealing the lie he tells Kurtz's Intended concerning his last words. Marlow, Stampfl asserts, "really believes in some of these lies (that is, in the saving power of 'efficiency')" in order to avoid "associations injurious to his ideal self-image."[16] Through repression Marlow thus uses language to "both cover up and reveal at the same moment."[17]

This deceptive use of language helps us to understand how one reader responds to Marlow's identification with the Russian sailor while another responds to his repudiation of the same character, for Marlow wishes, it seems, to reveal and simultaneously conceal his identification with the Russian in order to avoid acknowledging the depth of devotion to Kurtz he shares with his brother sailor. Indeed, Marlow and the Russian share far more than a spirit of adventure and an appreciation for Towson's *An Inquiry into Some Points of Seamanship*. Marlow accuses the Russian sailor of a lack of "meditation" over his devotion to Kurtz, yet Marlow's own meditation seems to occur only after Kurtz's death: "I had—for my sins—I suppose, to go through the ordeal of looking into it myself."[18] Indeed, Marlow silences the Russian sailor in order to evade the full knowledge of Kurtz's activities by shouting: "I don't want to know anything of the ceremonies used when approaching Mr. Kurtz."[19] And with his visit to the Intended Marlow fulfills his role as the last disciple of Kurtz: "I did not betray Mr. Kurtz—it was ordered I should never betray him—it was written I should be loyal to the nightmare of my choice."[20]

Marlow's concealment of his identification with the Russian sailor's devotion to Kurtz, ironically, also conceals his identification with the Russian's moral sense that Helder denies exists. This morality is displayed by the Russian's repayment of Van Shuyten's stake, by his disinterest in money and material possessions, by his use of firearms, as far as we know, solely to procure food for himself and the natives (whom he speaks with in their native tongue), by his refusal to participate in Kurtz's illicit activities, and by his tending to the ill Kurtz in the face of threats to his own life, going ten days without sleep. This last role of nurse to Kurtz is adopted by Marlow on the journey down the river. Marlow may snicker when the Russian says that he talked with Kurtz about "Everything! … Of love too,"[21] but the Russian's mind has been "enlarged" by the humanist, non-materialistic, spiritual values Kurtz came to the Congo to disseminate and which initially attract Marlow to Kurtz, not by the atrocities Kurtz has hypocritically committed. From this viewpoint, rather than neglecting "to hint however subtly or tentatively at an alternative frame of reference by which we may judge the actions and opinions of [Conrad's] characters," including Marlow, as Chinua Achebe accuses Conrad of doing in *Heart of Darkness*, Conrad hints at such a reference point in the character of the Russian sailor.[22]

What, then, are we to make of this harlequin in the heart of darkness? Into the gaps and ambiguities created by Marlow steps the reader, but interpreting the Russian harlequin as a symbol rather than as an archetype may exacerbate rather than resolve the "problem" Marlow is either unable or unwilling to solve himself. As a multivalent symbol, harlequin leads to an array of meanings ranging, as we have seen, from clown, court jester, fool, to "white aborigine" and "deformed simpleton," none of which is very satisfying when applied by itself to the Russian sailor. Viewing the Russian as an archetype rather than as a symbol, however, allows us to see him as representing a psychological pattern rather than as a signifier of one or more specific meanings. From this perspective, the Russian sailor is not a foil to Marlow but a prototype representing a stage of psychological development Marlow experiences through his journey into the heart of darkness and passes beyond.[23]

Jung's brief analysis of Harlequin focuses on the character as an archetype of initiation. According to Jung, Harlequin is an "ancient chthonic god,"[24] an identification that explicates on a mythological level the Russian sailor's presence at the Inner Station that is so inexplicable to Marlow. Jung cites Faust as a Harlequin who descends "to the crazy primitive world of the witches' sabbath,"[25] a descent traced by Marlow in his encounter with the two uncanny women, one with a cat on her lap and a wart on her nose, knitting black wool and "guarding the door of Darkness."[26] Yet even Jung seems left with more questions than answers as to the significance of Harlequin's descent:

Harlequin wanders like Faust through all these forms, though sometimes nothing betrays his presence but his wine, his lute, or the bright lozenges of his jester's costume. And what does he learn on his wild journey through man's millennial history? What quintessence will he distil from this accumulation of rubbish and decay, from these half-born or aborted possibilities of form and colour? What symbol will appear as the final cause and meaning of all this disintegration?[27]

Harlequin's journey, Jung argues, is "a descent into the cave of initiation and secret knowledge" leading to "the restoration of the whole man, by awakening the memories in the blood" of the "sinfully whole human being" symbolized for Faust by "Paris united with Helen,"

The *homo totus* who was forgotten when contemporary man lost himself in one-sidedness. It is he who at all times of upheaval has caused the tremor of the upper world, and always will. This man stands opposed to the man of the present, because he is the one who ever is as he was, whereas the other is what he is only for a moment. With my patients, accordingly, the katabasis and katalysis are followed by a recognition of the bipolarity of human nature and of the necessity of conflicting pairs of opposites. After the symbols of madness experienced during the period of disintegration there follow images which represent the coming together of the opposites: light/dark, above/below, white/black, male/female, etc.[28]

Harlequin's descent as an archetype for psychic disintegration and polarization into binary oppositions perhaps explains at least one puzzling aspect of the Russian sailor's behavior. For the often libidinous Harlequin, the Russian's hostility to the "wild and gorgeous apparition of a woman," presumably Kurtz's lover, whom the Russian sailor "would have tried to shoot" if she attempted to come aboard the steamer[29] seems out of character. The disintegration of binary opposites and their polarization may bring male and female into conflict and antagonism rather than into attraction and conciliation.

Much as heroes from Ajax to Luke Skywalker have left the protective world of the mother, Marlow's journey conforms to Jung's analysis of Harlequin's journey by tracing key elements of an archetypal initiation rite: separation, transformation, and return. The archetype of initiation is defined by Joseph L. Henderson as "the symbolic means by which the ego separates itself from the archetypes evoked by the parental images in early childhood." By such rites "young men and women are weaned away from their parents and forcibly made members of their clan or tribe. But in making this break with the childhood world, the original parent archetype will be injured, and the damage must be made good by a healing process of assimilation into the life of the group."[30] Just as the initiation journey often begins with the taking leave of the mother in order to uncover a secret truth, so Marlow takes leave of his symbolic mother, his ridiculed "excellent aunt."[31] His journey into the cave of initiation takes him into the heart of darkness where he witnesses both sides of human nature dissolved into separate components—the spiritual and physical, male and female, white and black—and receives a terrible secret knowledge summarized by Kurtz's last words: "The horror! The horror!"[32] Kurtz's last words are not solely a moral judgment passed on himself but an expression of the truth of human existence he has gained first hand and passes on to Marlow.

Subsequently, Marlow undergoes his own near-death experience, a symbolic psychic death and rebirth, before returning a changed man able to take his place in the tribe or community represented by the men in the Company to whom he tells his story aboard the *Nellie*. Along the way he finds himself back in "the sepulchral city resenting the sight of people hurrying through the streets to filch a little money from each other, to devour their infamous cookery, to gulp their unwholesome beer, to dream their insignificant and silly dreams."[33] Having glimpsed the Truth, Marlow thus returns to find, like Buddha before him, the materialistic life of the senses to be trivial and therefore spiritually unsatisfying after discovering, according to Jerome Thale, "not transcendent being but the heart of man."[34]

The Russian sailor as a Harlequin thus is an archetype for Marlow's descent into the heart of darkness, a psychic dissolution and disintegration symbolized by the distinct colors on the costume he wears, but where Marlow returns home transformed, the Russian sailor remains behind, slipping back into the darkness. To do otherwise would not be Harlequin, for he represents a stage rather than a goal. "This state of things in the psychic development of a patient is neither the end nor the goal," according to Jung. "It represents only a broadening of his outlook, which now embraces the whole of man's moral, bestial, and spiritual nature without as yet shaping it into a living unity."[35] The task of shaping such a unified, integrated identity falls not to the Russian sailor but to Marlow. Harlequin's costume carries the seeds of such an identity: "Harlequin is a tragically ambiguous figure, even though—as the initiated may discern—he already bears on his costume the symbols of the next stage of development. He is indeed the hero who must pass through the perils of Hades, but will he succeed?" asks Jung.[36]

According to the *Heart of Darkness*, success means shedding the role of Harlequin for that of Buddha.[37] Conrad insists on this symbolism in the descriptions of Marlow with which the story opens—"he had the pose of a Buddha preaching in European clothes and without a lotus-flower"[38]—and closes—"Marlow ceased, and sat apart, indistinct and silent, in the pose of a meditating Buddha."[39] Buddha, according to Joseph Campbell, is a classic example of the mythological hero whose journey takes him to the underworld where he retrieves a lost, secret knowledge—a boon—by which he is transformed and with which he returns and transforms the world:

> The Buddha's victory beneath the Bo Tree is the classic Oriental example of this deed. With the sword of his mind he pierced the bubble of the universe—and it shattered into naught. The whole world of natural experience, as well as the continents, heavens, and hells of traditional religious belief, exploded—together with their gods and demons. But the miracle of miracles was that though all exploded, all was nevertheless thereby renewed, revivified, and made glorious with the effulgence of true being. Indeed, the gods of the redeemed heavens raised their voices in harmonious acclaim of the man-hero who had penetrated beyond them to the void that was their life and source.[40]

Marlow as Buddha thus appears to complete successfully the initiation ritual. He penetrates to the void, learns "the horror," and returns to tell his companions aboard the *Nellie*.

If Marlow thus returns with the secret knowledge of *homo totus*, however, he shares it only with the men of the Company, an imperialist business venture that he still participates in. His rhetorical transformation of Kurtz's last words into a moral judgment Kurtz passes on himself—"an affirmation, a moral victory"[41]—relieves him of the duty to act upon his knowledge. Moreover, his refusal to share with women this knowledge leaves a disturbing aftertaste.

The lie he tells the Intended regarding Kurtz's last words denies her, and by extension all women, the benefit of the boon. She is thereby kept locked in a one-sided mode of consciousness which results in a state of eternal mourning, a death in life that, we recall Marlow saying, is the result of lies: "There is a taint of death, a flavour of mortality in lies—which is exactly what I hate and detest in the world—what I want to forget. It makes me miserable and sick, like biting something rotten would do."[42] Nevertheless, Marlow leaves the Intended in such a deathly state, leading to critical speculation as to his motivation. Clive Barnett, for example, believes Marlow does so to protect his masculine identity from what is perceived to be a devouring femininity symbolized by both the African woman and the Intended: "The lie emerges as the means by which Marlow's restraint finally secures his integrity by enabling him to resist this embrace of the feminine Other which mirrors that of the wilderness which was the undoing of Kurtz."[43]

Whatever the cause of the lie, Marlow's retelling of the story reveals that he cannot forget the rotten apple he has left in the Intended's mouth, thereby abandoning her to her sleep rather than awakening her, and neither can we readers. Though he returns from the underworld and transforms himself, the worlds of Belgium and London bear little signs of a corresponding revitalization and transformation. Indeed, his lie to the Intended insures that the imperialistic culture he professes to despise is maintained: "They—the women I mean—are out of it—should be out of it. We must help them to stay in that beautiful world of their own, lest ours gets worse."[44]

Consequently, Marlow's initiation remains incomplete and his success qualified, a Goodman Yellow rather than a Goodman Brown. By exchanging the costume of Harlequin for the costume of Buddha, Marlow does differentiate himself from the Russian sailor and passes beyond him psychologically. Where Marlow passes through the underworld and returns home with his gloomy boon, the Russian harlequin vanishes into the night where he belongs, wandering the Congo with his native friends, one red pocket bulging with cartridges, a dark blue one with Towson's inquiry, some English tobacco, and a used pair of shoes. Yet Marlow's final denial of the Russian harlequin is a denial of the *homo totus* Harlequin represents. Marlow asks, finally, "whether I had ever really seen him—whether it was possible to meet such a phenomenon!"[45] He is unable to recognize the self he met and left behind.

NOTES

1. C. G. Jung, *The Spirit in Man, Art, and Literature*, trans. R. F. C. Hull, Bollingen Series XX: *The Collected Works of C. G. Jung*, vol. 15 (Princeton: Princeton University Press, 1966), 140.

2. Joseph Conrad, *Heart of Darkness*. The Collected Works (1921, reprint *Heart of Darkness: A Case Study in Contemporary Criticism*, ed. Ross C. Murfin, New York: Bedford Books, 1989), 20.

3. Ibid., 70.

4. Ibid., 68.

5. Ibid., 68.

6. Ibid., 68.

7. Ibid., 22.

8. Ibid., 70.

9. Ibid., 74.

10. John W. Canario, "The Harlequin in *Heart of Darkness*," *Studies in Short Fiction*, 4 (1967): 225–33.

11. Jack Helder, "Fool Convention and Conrad's Hollow Harlequin," *Studies in Short Fiction*, 12 (1975): 361–8.

12. Ibid., 361–8.

13. For additional critical analyses of the Russian sailor see C. F. Burgess, "Conrad's Pesky Russian," *Nineteenth-Century Fiction*, 18 (1963): 189–93; and David Galef, "On the Margin: The Peripheral Characters in Conrad's *Heart of Darkness*," *Journal of Modern Literature*, 17, no. 1 (1990): 117–38.

14. Barry Stampfl, "Conrad's *Heart of Darkness*," *Explicator*, 49 no. 3 (1991): 162–5.

15. Conrad, *Heart*, 41.

16. Barry Stampfl, "Marlow's Rhetoric of (Self-) Deception in *Heart of Darkness*," *Modern Fiction Studies*, 37 no. 2 (1991): 183–96.

17. Stampfl, "Marlow's," 183–96.

18. Conrad, *Heart*, 82.

19. Ibid., 74.

20. Ibid., 80.

21. Ibid., 71.

22. Achebe argues that due to the absence of such a "hint" that Marlow's racial attitudes cannot be distinguished from Conrad's and therefore Conrad like Marlow is a "bloody racist" (788) in "An Image of Africa," *The Massachusetts Review*, 18 (1977): 782–94.

23. For a discussion of Marlow's adventure as a "discovery of the self" see Jerome Thale, "Marlow's Quest," *University of Toronto Quarterly* 24 (1955): 351–58; reprinted in part in Joseph Conrad, *Heart of Darkness: An Authoritative Text, Backgrounds and Sources, Essays in Criticism*, ed. Robert Kimbrough (New York: Norton, 1963) 181–6.

24. Jung, *Spirit*, 139.

25. Ibid., 139

26. Conrad, *Heart*, 25.

27. Jung, *Spirit*, 139.

28. Jung, Ibid., 139–40.

29. Conrad, *Heart*, 76–7.

30. Joseph L. Henderson, "Ancient Myths and Modern Man," *Man and His Symbols*, ed. Carl G. Jung (1964; reprint New York: Dell, 1968) 95–156.

31. Conrad, *Heart*, 26.

32. Ibid., 85.

33. Ibid., 87.

34. Jerome Thale, "Marlow's Quest," *University of Toronto Quarterly* 24 (1955): 351–58. Reprint in part in Joseph Conrad, *Heart of Darkness: An Authoritative Text, Backgrounds and Sources, Essays in Criticism*, ed. Robert Kimbrough (New York: Norton, 1963) 181–6.

35. Jung, *Spirit*, 140.

36. Ibid., 140.

37. See William Bysshe Stein, "The Lotus Posture and *Heart of Darkness*," *Modern Fiction Studies*, 2 (Winter 1956–7): 167–70; and Robert O. Evans, "A Further Comment on '*Heart of Darkness*,'" *Modern Fiction Studies*, 3 (Winter 1957–8): 358–60. Both are available in Joseph Conrad, *Heart of Darkness: An Authoritative Text, Backgrounds and Sources, Essays in Criticism*, ed. Robert Kimbrough (New York: Norton, 1963) 196–99 and 202–4.

38. Conrad, *Heart*, 21.

39. Ibid., 94.

40. Joseph Campbell, *The Hero with a Thousand Faces*, 2nd ed. Bollingen Series 17 (Princeton: Princeton University Press 1968) 191–2.

41. Conrad, *Heart*, 87.

42. Ibid., 41–2.

43. Clive Barnett, "'A Choice of Nightmares': Narration and Desire in *Heart of Darkness*," *Gender, Place, & Culture*, 3 no. 3 (1996): 277–91.

44. Conrad, *Heart*, 63.

45. Ibid., 79.

PADMINI MONGIA

The Rescue: Conrad, Achebe, and the Critics

I am interested in touching upon numerous concerns raised by *Heart of Darkness*, all of which radiate around the fraught issue of race and its construction in the novel. For many Conradians, this issue boils down to the charge of racism leveled against the novel, and Conrad, most prominently by Chinua Achebe. Achebe wrote his essay now over twenty years ago. Since it was published, there have been several responses that have apparently revealed the many problems with his argument to demonstrate solidly its ineffectuality.[1] Many of these responses are developed in terms of an opposition between the African author who speaks out of his "race"—therefore only with hostility— and the critical expert—the "objective" European critic. These responses are therefore mounted in terms of Achebe's "misrepresentation" of Conrad's text; in terms of Conrad's difference from other European authors at the time; and in terms of the invalidity of bringing a contemporary understanding of race and racism—assumed uncritically to be a progress over the past—to bear on a text of the 1890s. First, I want to unravel some aspects of these responses and examine the structures they rely on. Next, I want to ask why, given the apparently extremely ill-thought-out bases of Achebe's argument, do Conradians continue to "answer" him?[2]

My point of entry into the discussion of race in *Heart of Darkness* is not an attempt to lay to rest the question whether or not Conrad was a racist,

From *Conradiana* 33, no. 2 (2001): 153–163. © 2001 by Texas Tech University Press.

even if such a project were possible. So, I do not intend to work through Achebe's specific charges and the responses to them with the aim of showing the rightness or wrongness of either. Instead I want to use the responses to Achebe's essay in order to enter a different kind of discussion, one that will enable us, by our addressing the assumptions behind these critiques, to view his charge of racism from a fresh perspective. I should clarify immediately that the essays I am considering here are those that choose to respond to Achebe directly and not the many other works that address race, empire, and colony in increasingly more novel and challenging ways.[3] I should also clarify that throughout this essay, when I say the Euro-American academy, I am referring not only to the geographical regions evoked by the term but also to a strain of critical inquiry that is found as much in South Africa and India as it is in Pennsylvania and Stockholm. What I am referring to is an epistemological rather than a geographical position. It is not easy, of course, to categorize this strain without resorting to gross simplifications, but I hope, as I proceed, that some of the assumptions and approaches that help define this academy will become clearer.

To begin with, let me sum up what I see as the main concern of Achebe's argument. In his essay "An Image of Africa," initially presented as the Chancellor's Lecture at the University of Massachusetts in 1975, Achebe uses *Heart of Darkness* to develop the following argument: that there is "the desire—one might indeed say the need—in western psychology to set Africa up as a foil to Europe, a place of negations at once remote and vaguely familiar in comparison with which Europe's own state of spiritual grace will be manifest."[4] Achebe makes this point early in the essay and arrives at it via two episodes; the first is an encounter with an older man who expresses wonder and surprise at the very notion of African literature. The second moment is a letter from a high school student expressing delight that Achebe's novel, *Things Fall Apart*, taught him about the "customs and superstitions of an African tribe" (782). In this second episode, Achebe stresses the unquestioned Western assumption that tribes are to be found elsewhere, particularly in Africa. Both these moments Achebe sees as symptomatic of the Western psychological need to set Africa up as a place of negations. Only via his interest in this larger argument does he approach Conrad and *Heart of Darkness*; he does so to explore this symptom in more detail, this time as a novelist reading a novel. I have spent so much time on this opening because it is important, I think, to view Achebe's entire essay, including his charge that "Conrad was a bloody racist," within the larger context Achebe is at some pains to establish.

Why does Achebe choose *Heart of Darkness* as opposed to some other novel which might just as well or better demonstrate his case? The reason is crucial, I think, to an understanding of his main concern. Achebe says: "Conrad . . . is undoubtedly one of the great stylists of modern fiction and a good storyteller into the bargain. His contribution therefore falls automatically into a different class—permanent literature—read and taught and constantly evaluated by serious academics" (783). Conrad's place, as Achebe suggests, in the canon of high literature is so secure that it insulates the novel against the kind of polemical reading Achebe mounts. Subsequent responses to his essay might well be read as only underscoring his point.

Let us now glance at some of the responses to Achebe. There are many, many essays that set out to undermine Achebe's reading. Here I will focus chiefly on Hunt Hawkins's "The Issue of Racism in *Heart of Darkness*" and also Cedric Watts's "A Bloody Racist: About Achebe's View of Conrad." Hawkins's essay is short, with a series of "defenses" of Conrad, and utilizes all those features that we see in other responses to Achebe as well. His essay is therefore a sort of ur-example of the kind of approach I am interested in examining and offers me a convenient anchor through what follows next. Watts's essay, too, is an important response to Achebe, a fact well-underscored by its inclusion in the Critical Assessments series edited by Keith Carabine.[5]

The main perspective that critics use to frame their response to Achebe is the idea that he reduces the complexity of Conrad's novel by his mean-minded appraisal of its construction of race. Hawkins's essay begins with this point, although he arrives at it after granting Achebe some validity. Hawkins says that an argument such as Achebe's brings "a fresh perspective to Conrad studies," carries "a measure of truth," and that "the image which Conrad projects of African life could hardly be called flattering" (163). In the very next sentence, though, Hawkins goes on to say that "it is overly severe simply to write Conrad off as a racist" (163). Instead, Hawkins suggests that a better understanding of Conrad's "complexity" can be reached by "studying the series of defenses which can, and have, and should be offered on his behalf" (164–165). Immediately, then, before we even begin the critique of Achebe, a certain structure has been put in place. This structure posits Achebe and his position as "simplistic" against which is pitted the complexity of not only Conrad but the Conradian critic responsive to this complexity and therefore one able to reproduce it in his reading. Conrad and the appropriate critic then join forces in order to undermine Achebe's reading.[6]

How indeed does Hawkins arrive at the charge that Achebe "simply writes Conrad off as a racist?" If indeed Achebe were doing so, would he spend the better part of an essay on the enterprise? Would he not dismiss Conrad as he does other writers, for instance, and thereby write Conrad off? In fact, I would suggest that because Achebe *cannot* simply write Conrad off as a racist, he writes his critical essay in the first place. My summary of Achebe's essay earlier demonstrates, I think, that because Achebe takes Conrad and his work seriously, no such simple "writing off" is possible at all. Further, Hawkins's swift but certain move to reduce Achebe's essay to a simple "writing off" illustrates the point Achebe tries to make in his essay: that Conrad's place in the canon of high-literature is so secure that it blinds the reader and critic to the operations of racism in the text. It seems that in mainstream Conrad criticism, a charge such as racism can only be approached as a sign of a simple reductive reading as opposed to a valid approach, one amongst many, surely, but nevertheless valid, that a critical reader might bring to the novel.

In a similar vein, Cedric Watts's argument is peppered with statements that essentially reduce Achebe's position to simple-mindedness. So, Watts says: "In *Things Fall Apart*, Achebe showed himself capable of fine discriminations; it is a pity that that capacity appears to have been eroded by bitterness" (406). Other comments such as "spleen has clouded his judgement" or that Achebe is "unable to perceive" (410) only perpetuate a structure in which the critic who sees racism as a valuable charge is reduced to being blinded by external pressures so that the complexity of the text, and indeed of its possible readings, is evaded. Why is it that the charge of racism has to be reduced to a simplification as indeed no other kind of critical approach does? How many papers have we all read on *Heart of Darkness* with titles such as "Marlow as Buddha: Wisdom or Perversion," or "Marlow's Journey to Hades," or "Colour Imagery in *Heart of Darkness*," or "The Heart of Horror" or even "The Art of Horror" etc.?[7] Why is it that all these works and their limited interests can be seen as contributing to the body of knowledge on *Heart of Darkness* without it being necessary to dismiss the readings as simplistic? Why, then, is racism seen as the sole issue that reduces the text as opposed to being one valid perspective on certain aspects of the novel?

To develop further the "simplicity" of Achebe's argument, critics resort to another gesture familiar in almost all critiques of Achebe's essay. This gesture relies on the use of another "Third World" writer or critic, with a view opposed to Achebe's, to suggest that his perspective is indeed mean-minded. Hawkins, therefore, relies on the Kenyan novelist Leonard Kibera, who says "I study *Heart of Darkness* as an examination of the West itself and not as a comment on Africa" (Hawkins 64). Further on in the essay, Hawkins quotes the positive comments made by the Sri Lankan critic D. C. R. A. Goonetilleke and the black South African Ezekiel Mphahlele as additional evidence that Achebe's view is jaundiced. Similarly, Watts says, "I have taken heart from my acquaintance Lewis Nkosi, the black playwright and critic, who has worked on Conrad with me at Sussex" (405). What is the interest in quoting other "Third World" voices here? The argument is unstated but is in fact quite clear. Other "Third World" writers, all immediately assumed to have a critical understanding and interest in questions of race and racism, do not think Conrad racist. Therefore, Achebe is hostile and blinkered. What is troublesome in this sort of move is the essentializing of race the gesture relies on. Basically, this essentializing suggests that only blacks and browns can address meaningfully what is or is not racist. Therefore, since several "colored" folk have found Conrad praiseworthy, Achebe's position is by no means valid. This strategy enables an evasion of Achebe's argument while his position is undermined by pitting one Third-World voice against another, and where it is already clear which perspective we are supposed to find limited.

Let us consider some of the assumptions that go into such a move. I think it is clear that the evocation of Third-World voices is necessary for these critics because *all* folks from the Third World are supposed to be interested in and critical of issues of race and racism. They are also supposed to, instinctually, have greater access to these nuances. The issue of racism, therefore, is made into an instinctual field, an issue that is felt or unfelt depending on the color of the critic. Questions surrounding racism are thus denied any scholarly validity; if color determines one's knowledge then surely the realm of research and study in understanding racism has been effectively bypassed.

Watts says: "Achebe is black and I am white. . . . There seems to be an insinuation, as Achebe proceeds, that whites are disqualified on racial grounds from judging the text" (405). Where is this insinuation in Achebe's argument? Yes, Achebe suggests that white racism against Africa is such a normal way of thinking that its operations are completely missed in a text such as *Heart of Darkness*. But from this point, how do we get to the insinuation that whites are disqualified from judging the text? To my mind, we don't. Instead, it seems to me that Achebe presents his argument precisely in order to jostle the white establishment into a consideration of race that would allow them to see its operations even in texts considered high literature. But a move such as Watts's, I think, perpetuates a dangerous distinction between black and white and virtually implies that there are areas of critical study intrinsic to different color groups. Surely if Achebe is arguing that only blacks are qualified to comment on race in *Heart of Darkness*, there is no room at all for any kind of dialogue or debate and he might just as well not have bothered writing his essay at all. This essentializing of racial difference and the critical knowledge it apparently brings in its wake only makes it impossible to disagree with Achebe's charge that the West produces and reproduces a racial "Other" against which it can profitably measure itself.

Further, when white critics say, as some do, that they are not equipped to talk of race because they are white, an absolute and final marginalization of the issue is being undertaken. A tremendous and dangerous abdication of responsibility is going on here. Not only is whiteness also a construct, but much recent critical work addresses this construction in ways which allow access to the cultural and sociological pressures that determine it.[8] So, certainly the very notion of whiteness as somehow a given needs to be questioned. And the critic who absolves himself or herself of the authority for a meaningful engagement with the question of race is the critic who refuses to hear an

Achebe and who contributes, ironically, to exactly the kind of problem a text
such as *Heart of Darkness* poses.

A further defense Hawkins and others offer is that although Africans
are presented as negative, so too are Europeans, in fact even more so. What
is the nature of this defense? Does the fact that Conrad casts a critical eye
upon all he surveys exonerate him from Achebe's charge, even if we agreed
that this eye was impartial in its critique or even in the balance more critical
of Europeans? I think not. For surely the point that Conrad has his problems
with Europeans and their greed and excesses cannot neutralize the case
Achebe and others make regarding his racist view towards Africans? This
sort of argument refuses to take on the reasons why Achebe argues for the
dehumanization of blacks, which Hawkins himself, as I have pointed out,
could agree with in part. If we can agree that Conrad's presentation of Africans
is selectively and specifically derogatory, as his presentation of Europeans is
not, then surely suggesting an equivalence between his representations of
both groups is deliberately naive.

Another common argument along the same lines states that Conrad
proffers many positive comments on Africans which Achebe chooses to
ignore. Cedric Watts finds some of these moments in Conrad's presentation
of Africans as "vital" in sharp contrast to the "hollow" Europeans. Watts says
that, far from dehumanizing blacks as Achebe suggests, Conrad presents
them as "by far the happiest, healthiest, and most vital" (407). However, as
much recent work on colonial discourse has shown us, vitality and naturalness
are by no means unqualified positive statements. Quite the contrary. Let us
remember that this "naturalness" of the "native" was one of the chief arguments
that justified the civilizing mission of the Europeans, for it was this natural
vital energy that needed to be reined in. One of the commonest tropes in
colonial discourse pits the knowledge/power of the European against the
natural, instinctual, purely physical energy of the native. How then can we
celebrate the vitality of the Africans in the novel?

The most important argument made against Achebe is the one that
states that Conrad was ahead of his time. Cedric Watts says: "If Achebe had
but recalled that *Heart of Darkness* appeared in 1899, when Victoria was on
the throne, when imperialistic fervour was extreme and the Boer War soon to
begin, he might have been more prepared to recognize various unconventional
qualities of Conrad's tale" (406). Hawkins argues that Marlow learns to
recognize the humanity of the Africans, and that "such a recognition on the
part of Marlow, and Conrad, was remarkable for his era" (168). At the same
time, this argument also resorts to placing Conrad in his time. Hawkins,
therefore, quoting Sarvan, says Conrad "was not entirely immune to the
infection of the beliefs and attitudes of his age" but he was "ahead of most
in trying to break free" (169). Robert Hampson points out that the readers

of *Blackwood's Magazine*, where the story first appeared, would have been, like Marlow's audience on the *Nellie*, made up of males of the colonial class whose attitudes would be fairly predictable. Hampson argues that Conrad therefore shapes his story with this audience in mind. Let us accept these positions and accept that, given Conrad's moment, it is hardly surprising that the text reflects certain attitudes and that Conrad, by proffering a critique of at least some aspects of imperialism, undermines any simple celebration of it. However, there are two parts to this argument: the one stressing Conrad's difference from other writers of the 1890s, and the other stressing the many codes he shared with them. For an understanding of Achebe and specifically his charge of racism, it seems to me obvious that we must consider the second of these positions. For if we accept Conrad's historical and cultural location, must we not also accept that his views are shaped by that moment and indeed the very ontological possibilities available to him in the 1890s? To my mind, not acknowledging this locatedness, with its constraints that we may now find troubling, is to force Conrad and his text into a dangerous aspecificity.

What is at stake if we agreed with Achebe that Conrad was a racist? Usually, critics tend to find it *reductive* that we bring to Conrad a perspective tinged by our own times and our apparently more progressive attitudes towards race and difference. So, the argument goes, is it not unfair that we read Conrad after, for instance, having read Achebe? Watts says, "Marlow, however, cannot be blamed for lacking the benefit of *Things Fall Apart*, which appeared nearly sixty years after he told his tale" (408). How could one argue against Watts here? But at the same time, surely it behooves us, as readers of *Heart of Darkness* almost a hundred years after it first appeared, to read from our times? If these times are supposed to be an advance over the sort of reductive thinking of a century ago, then surely we should be able to call a work racist because we think it is so, without claiming that some abhorrent and irreparable damage has been done to the institutions of high culture.

But therein lies the rub, because the problem with accepting *Heart of Darkness* as relying on dangerous racist tropes threatens the august institutions of high culture. And this threat, in the twenty years since Achebe wrote his essay, has only increased. How else can we understand the constant need to write back to him? Achebe's essay on *Heart of Darkness* is by no means the final or best word on the constructions of race in Conrad. Especially now, it is only one work amongst many that deals with the question of race in the novel. Yet he remains the critic to be responded to, as is amply demonstrated by Phil Joffe's essay at the 1991 Poland conference, subsequently published in the proceedings in 1993. Joffe's essay, too, approaches the question of race in the terms that have been relied on by Conradians since Achebe first published his piece. So, we find the familiar polarity between the simplicity of Achebe's position against which is pitted the "complexity of Conrad's text,"[9] a complexity that Joffe's students also seem to divine, for he says students "register the ambivalences and contradictions in Marlow's discourse without concluding that Conrad has a racist agenda" (84). Given that Joffe teaches in South Africa, to a diverse group of students, the effect this statement is supposed to have is clear.

If indeed the bases of Achebe's argument are entirely too simplistic, why has it not been possible to dismiss his essay entirely? The fact that Achebe is a prominent writer is not enough of an answer, for surely there are many other instances where prominent writers have written pieces that have not been considered worth the kind of debate Achebe has generated? Not only has this not been the case but Achebe's argument seems to have offered the most commonly used structure for approaching race in the novel. Anybody who works on Conrad and/or teaches *Heart of Darkness* in the Anglo-American academy (and beyond) is by now familiar with Achebe's 1975 essay and his infamous charge that Conrad was "a bloody racist." While Achebe's 1978 piece revised the phrase to read, "Conrad was a thoroughgoing racist," the former phrase has become an almost as entrenched quotation as Conrad's own "the horror, the horror." With the inclusion of Achebe's essay in the Norton Critical edition of 1988, Achebe's perspective has become virtually as canonized as Conrad's novel, so that Conrad and Achebe are often taught in the Euro-American academy alongside each other. Now that *Heart of Darkness* is taught virtually inseparably from the Achebe essay, one could read the inclusion of Achebe in college curricula to signify an acknowledgment, albeit uneasy, of the significance of addressing race when exploring the novella. Yet I would like us to consider the inclusion of Achebe's essay as an instance of the marginalization of race as a significant theoretical issue in the teaching of literature.

Achebe deploys a certain train of binary thinking in his essay, with the intent, I think, of shocking and deliberately provoking the critical establishment. Ironically, though, his provocation has led the mainstream Euro-American academy to engage with the question of race, racism, and racial difference in Conrad only in terms that perpetuate and indeed strengthen these binary distinctions. Achebe's essay was presented in 1975, long before the canon wars and long before post-colonial readings gained a firm ground. It is not surprising that Achebe's essay is deliberately meant to provoke. But how do we explain the obsessive need not only to respond to Achebe but to do so only in terms that solidify differences between black and white, between simplicity and complexity, between the appropriate historical or ahistorical readings? I think only if we accept a refusal on the part of this academy to allow race and its constructions to be anything other than reductive approaches. Because Achebe's famous charge can be read as "extreme," it becomes possible to dismiss his argument rather than take it seriously. Rarely does the critic consider the larger argument Achebe is trying to mount, which he establishes at the beginning of his essay.

Heart of Darkness is a text read and evaluated constantly. In order to understand Achebe's frustrated rage and indeed to understand the politics of race surrounding the novel, the fact that *Heart of Darkness* exists as a "classic" cannot be ignored. A "classic" in its materiality exists quite differently than, say, a work like Haggard's *King Solomon's Mines*. As a text of high modernism and a work considered "among the half-dozen greatest short novels in the English novel" (Achebe 783), *Heart of Darkness* also needs to be approached in terms of its popularity in literature courses in Europe, America, and India. The text has a life much larger than the story it apparently tells, and this larger life forces us to pause and consider the kind of weight a "classic" carries, the making of canons, and the role of the critic and the teacher in the production and perpetuation of canons and of their sacrosanct status. All these aspects of *Heart of Darkness*'s iconic status cannot be ignored for a full understanding of why the discussions of race and racism in the novel have been so charged and virulent.

The canonization of Achebe's "An Image of Africa" sets the terms and limits of discussions of race and empire in Anglo-American college classrooms. The inclusion of Achebe in the critical canon allows us to find ourselves within a familiar Conradian structure, a structure where Conrad needs to be rescued by the complex critic from the contaminated space of "racism" and brought back firmly to the world of high literature. For clearly we are on a battlefield. Hawkins, remember, felt it necessary to offer defenses on Conrad's behalf. The situation might be described something like this: Conrad has been attacked, he is under siege, and rescue is necessary. Defenses must be proffered, and who better to do so than the critic who has access to his complexity because, indeed, he shares it. This is a structure that Conradian critics are familiar with, evoking as it does those Conradian structures "between men." I am thinking here of the group on the *Nellie*, or the recurring construction of "us" that patterns *Lord Jim*. Several critics have argued for Marlow's need to rescue a Jim or a Kurtz for this world of men. This pattern is echoed in the structure of rescue I've been exploring, where the Conrad critic needs to rescue Conrad and his text from the charge of "racism" in order to bring him back to the canon of "high" art, where "racism" needs must have a more shadowy and contested existence.

NOTES

1. In this essay, I consider primarily Cedric Watts's "'A Bloody Racist': About Achebe's View of Conrad," in *Joseph Conrad: Critical Assessments*, ed. Keith Carabine (Sussex: Helm Information, 1992), 2:405–18 and Hunt Hawkins's "The Issue of Racism in

Heart of Darkness," *Conradiana* 14.3 (1982): 163–71. In addition to these essays by Watts and Hawkins, other responses to Achebe include C. P. Sarvan's "Racism and the *Heart of Darkness,*" *International Fiction Review* 7.1 (1980): 6–10; Robert Hampson's essay "'Heart of Darkness' and 'The Speech that Cannot Be Silenced,'" *English: Journal of the English Association* 39.163 (Spring 1990): 15–32; and Bruce E. Fleming's "Brothers Under the Skin: Achebe on *Heart of Darkness,*" *College Literature* 19/20 (Oct. 92/Feb.93): 90–9. Subsequent references to the Hampson, Hawkins, and Watts essays will be cited parenthetically within the text.

2. I want to thank Jakob Lothe for inviting me to speak on Achebe in Oslo in 1996. I appreciate responses I received there from him, Cedric Watts, Jeremy Hawthorn, and Andrew Roberts.

3. I am thinking here of work such as Chris Bongie's *Exotic Memories* (Stanford: Stanford University Press, 1991) or Christopher Gogwilt's *Joseph Conrad and the Invention of the West* (Stanford: Stanford University Press, 1995), which approach imperialism, colonialism, and racism by taking into account a range of historical and sociological complexity. It is also only fair to point out that the positions taken by Hawkins and Watts in the essays I discuss here do not represent both critics' substantive work historicizing and politicizing readings of Conrad.

4. Chinua Achebe, "An Image of Africa," *The Massachusetts Review* 18.4 (Winter 1977), 783. Subsequent citations are in parentheses in the text.

5. The Critical Assessments series makes a significant contribution to the production of a canon of Conrad criticism. The monumental four-volume set contains a separate segment devoted to *Heart of Darkness* with the following subtitle: "Race, Imperialism and the Third World." The confluence of terms here only underscores my argument later in this essay that matters of "race" are perceived by the critical establishment as separate from "critical," "literary" assessments. Only such an understanding helps me explain the place and position of the "third world" in the title. See Keith Carabine, ed., *Joseph Conrad: Critical Assessments*, 4 vols. (Sussex: Helm Information, 1992).

6. My argument has been sharpened by Hunt Hawkins' responses to both an oral and written version of this paper. I am grateful to him for the careful reading and commentary he offered on an earlier version of this essay. Our dialogue has led both of us to complicate our readings of Achebe and of the critics. Were we to write our respective essays today, neither of us would do so in their current form/s since we would both be posing different questions.

7. All these titles have, of course, been fabricated.

8. See, for instance, Toni Morrison's *Playing in the Dark* (Cambridge, MA: Harvard University Press, 1992), a provocative examination of the Africanist presence in American literature. See also Ruth Frankenberg's work on the construction of whiteness and several recent issues of *American Quarterly* devoted to the topic.

9. Phil Joffe, "Africa and Joseph Conrad's *Heart of Darkness*: The 'bloody racist' (?) as Demystifier of Imperialism," in *Conrad's Literary Career* (Conrad: Eastern and Western Perspectives, Vol. 1), eds. Keith Carabine, Owen Knowles, Wieslaw Krajka (Boulder: East European Monographs, 1993) 75–90. Subsequent references to this essay appear parenthetically.

J. HILLIS MILLER

Should We Read "Heart of Darkness"?

The inaccessible incites from its place of hiding.

(Jacques Derrida)

Should we read "Heart of Darkness?" May we read it? Must we read it? Or, on the contrary, ought we not to read it or allow our students and the public in general to read it? Should every copy be taken from all the shelves and burned? What or who gives us the authority to make a decision about that? Who is this "we" in whose name I speak? What community forms that "we?" Nothing could be more problematic than the bland appeal to some homogeneous authoritative body, say professors of English literature everywhere, capable of deciding collectively whether "we" should read "Heart of Darkness." By "read" I mean not just run the words passively through the mind's ear, but perform a reading in the strong sense, an active responsible response that renders justice to a book by generating more—language in its turn the language of attestation, even though that—language may remain silent or implicit. Such a response testifies to having it been changed by the reading.

Part of the problem, as you can see, is that it is impossible to decide authoritatively whether or not we should read "Heart of Darkness" without reading it in that strong sense. By then it is too late. I have already read it, been affected by it, and passed my judgment, perhaps recorded it for others

From *Conrad in Africa: New Essays on "Heart of Darkness,"* pp. 21–40. © 2002 by Maria Curie–Sklodowska University, Lublin.

to read. Which of us, however, would or should want to take someone else's word for what is in a book?

Each must read again in his or her turn and bear witness to that reading in his or her turn. In that aphorism about which Jacques Derrida has had so much to say, Paul Celan says, "No one bears witness for the witness." This might be altered to say, "No one can do your reading for you." Each must read for himself or herself and testify anew. This structure is inscribed in "Heart of Darkness" itself. The primary narrator bears witness through exact citation to what he heard Marlow say that night on the deck of cruising yawl *Nellie*, as he and the other men, the Lawyer, the Accountant, the Director of Companies, representatives of advanced capitalism and imperialism, waited for the tide to turn so they could float down the Thames and out to sea, presumably on a pleasure cruise.[1] They have enough wealth and leisure to take time off to do as an aesthetic end in itself what Marlow has done for pay as a professional seaman. The profession of the primary, framing narrator is never specified. He cites with what the reader is led to believe is conscientious and meticulous accuracy just what Marlow said. What Marlow said, put within quotation marks throughout, is a story, the recounting of and accounting for what he calls an "experience" that "seemed somehow to throw a kind of light on everything about me—and into my thoughts. It was sombre enough, too—and pitiful—not extraordinary in any way—not very clear either. No not very clear, and yet it seemed to throw a kind of light" ("Heart of Darkness," *YS*, 51). That recounting and accounting centers on an attempt to "render justice," as Marlow puts it, to Kurtz, the man he meets at "the farthest point of navigation and the culminating point of my experience." What Marlow says at the beginning is also an implicit promise to his listeners and to us as readers. He promises that he will pass on to them and to us the illumination he has received.

Nor have Conrad's readers failed to respond to this demand for interpretation. A large secondary literature has sprung up around "Heart of Darkness." These essays and books of course have a constative dimension. They often provide precious information about Conrad's life, about his experiences in Africa, about late nineteenth-century imperialism, especially about that terrible murdering devastation wrought by King Leopold in the Belgian Congo, as it was then called, about the supposed "originals" of characters in "Heart of Darkness," and so on. This secondary literature, however, often also has an explicit performative dimension. Conrad's novella is brought before the bar of justice, arraigned, tried, and judged. The critic acts as witness of his or her reading, also as interrogator, prosecuting attorney, jury, and presiding judge. The critic passes judgment and renders justice. "Heart of Darkness" has often received a heavy sentence from its critics. It has been condemned, often in angry terms, as racist or sexist, sometimes in the same essay as both. Examples are the influential essay of 1975 by the distinguished Nigerian novelist, Chinua Achebe ("Conrad was a bloody racist") or an essay of 1989 by Bette London: "Dependent upon unexamined assumptions, themselves culturally suspect, the novel, in its representations of sex and gender, supports dubious cultural claims; it participates in and promotes a racial as well as gender ideology that the narrative represents as transparent and 'self-evident.'"[2] Edward Said's judgment in *Culture and Imperialism*, though giving Conrad his due as a critic of imperialism and recognizing the complexity of doing justice to "Heart of Darkness," is in the end equally severe in his summing up: "The cultural and ideological evidence that Conrad was wrong in his Eurocentric way is both impressive and rich."[3]

These are powerful indictments. If what they say renders justice to "Heart of Darkness," if their witness may be trusted, it might seem inevitably to follow that the novella should not be read, taught, or written about, except perhaps as an example of something detestable. Nevertheless, according to the paradox I have already mentioned, you could only be sure about this by reading the novella yourself, thereby putting yourself, if these critics are right, in danger of becoming sexist, racist, and Eurocentric yourself.

Even so, no one bears witness for the witness, and no one else can do your reading for you. To pass judgment anew it is necessary to take the risk and read "Heart of Darkness" for yourself. I shall now try to do that. I begin by claiming that "Heart of Darkness" is a literary work, not history, autobiography, travel writing, journalism, or any other genre.

In just what way does "Heart of Darkness" invite reading as literature rather than, say, as a historical account or as an autobiography? The most obvious way is in the displacement from Conrad to two imaginary narrators, neither of whom is to be identified with Conrad, any more than Socrates, in the Platonic dialogues is to be identified with Plato. The reader who says Conrad speaks directly for himself either in the words of the frame narrator or in Marlow's words does so at his or her peril and in defiance of the most elementary literary conventions. Whatever the frame narrator or Marlow says is ironized or suspended, presented implicitly in parabasis, by being presented as the speech of an imaginary character.

A second way "Heart of Darkness" presents itself as literature is in the elaborate tissue of figures and other rhetorical devices that make up, so to speak, the texture of the text. The simplest and most obvious of these devices is the use of similes, signalled by "like" or "as." These similes displace things that are named by one or the other of the narrators and asserts that they are like something else. This something else forms a consistent subtext or counterpoint defining everything that can be seen as a veil hiding something more truthful or essential behind.

The first use of the figure of screens that are lifted to reveal more screens behind, in a structure that is apocalyptic in the etymological sense of "unveiling," as well as in the sense of having to do with death, judgment, and other last things, comes when the frame narrator, describing the evening scene just before sunset, when the sky is "a benign immensity of unstained light" (46) as it looks from the *Nellie* at anchor in the Thames estuary, says: "the very mist on the Essex marshes *was like* a gauzy and radiant fabric, hung from the wooded rises inland; and draping the low shores in diaphanous folds" (46—emphasis JHM). These similes, as they follow in a line punctuating the text at rhythmic intervals, are not casual or fortuitous. They form a system, a powerful undertext beneath the first-level descriptive language. They invite the reader to see whatever either of the narrators sees and names on the first level of narration as a veil or screen hiding something invisible or not yet visible behind it, though when each veil is lifted it uncovers only another veil behind it, according to a paradox essential to the genre of the apocalypse. Apocalypse: the word means "unveiling" in Greek. If one had to name the genre to which "Heart of Darkness" belongs the answer would be that it is a failed apocalypse, or, strictly speaking, since all apocalypses ultimately fail to lift the last veil, it is just that, a member of the genre apocalypse. The film modelled on "Heart of Darkness," *Apocalypse Now*, was brilliantly and accurately named, except for that word "now." Apocalypse is never now. It is always to come, a thing of the future, both infinitely distant and immediately imminent.

In "Heart of Darkness," it is, to borrow Conrad's own words, as if each episode were like "some sordid *farce* acted in front of a sinister back-cloth" (61—emphasis JHM). The novella is structured as a long series of episodes each one of which appears with extreme vividness before the reader's imaginary vision, brought there by Conrad's remarkable descriptive power, only to vanish and be replaced by the next, as though a figured screen had been lifted to reveal yet another figured screen behind it, with the darkness behind all, like that "sinister back-cloth" Marlow names.

A third distinctively literary feature of "Heart of Darkness" has already been named. The novella is ironic through and through. The reader might wish this were not the case and deplore Conrad's radical irony, but there it is, an indubitable fact. "Heart of Darkness" is a masterwork of irony, as when the eloquent idealism of Kurtz's pamphlet on "The Suppression of Savage Customs" is undercut by the phrase scrawled at the bottom: "Exterminate all the brutes!" or as the dying Africans in the "grove of death" are called "helpers" in the great "work" of civilizing the continent (66). Marlow's narrative in particular is steeped in irony throughout. The problem is that it is impossible to be certain how to take that irony. Irony is, as Hegel and Kierkegaard said, "infinite absolute negativity," or as Friedrich Schlegel said, a "permanent parabasis," a continuous suspension of clearly identifiable meaning. It is a principle of unintelligibility, or, in Schlegel's words, "*Unverstundlichkeit*." Irony is a constant local feature of Marlow's narrative style—saying one thing and meaning another; as when the Europeans at the Central Station engaged in the terrible work of imperialist conquest, the "merry dance of death and trade" are said to be, in yet another simile, like "pilgrims": "They wandered here and there with their absurd long staves *in* their hands, like a lot of faithless pilgrims bewitched inside a rotten fence" (76—emphasis JHM). This stylistic undercutting *is* mimed in that larger structure in which each episode *is* replaced by the next, so that each is suspended by the reader's knowledge that it is only a contemporary appearance, not some ultimate goal of revelation attained. Each is certain to vanish and be replaced by the next scene to be enacted before that sinister black back-cloth.

A fourth ostentatious literary feature of "Heart of Darkness" is the recurrent *prosopopoeias*, the personifications of the darkness (whatever that word means here). This begins in the title. The darkness has a "heart." *Prosopopoeia* is the ascription of a name, a face, or a voice to the absent, the inanimate, or the dead. By a speech act, a performative utterance, *prosopopoeia* creates the fiction of a personality where in reality there is none. All *prosopopoeias* are also *catachreses*. They move the verbal fiction of a personality over to name something unknown/unknowable, and therefore, strictly speaking, unnamable in any literal language, something radically other than human personality: something absent, inanimate, or dead. It is no accident that so many traditional examples of *catachresis* are also personifications: "headland," "face of a mountain," "tongue of land," "table leg." "Heart of Darkness" is another such *catachrestic prosopopoeia*, to give it its barbarous-sounding Greek rhetorical name. We project our own bodies on the landscape and on surrounding artifacts. We give the darkness a heart. In "Heart of Darkness" *prosopopoeias* are a chief means of naming by indirection what Conrad calls, in a misleading and inadequate metaphor, "the darkness," or "the wilderness," or, most simply and perhaps most truthfully, "it." More than a dozen explicit personifications of this something, that is not really a person but an "it," asexual or transsexual, impersonal, indifferent, though to Marlow it seems like a person, rhythmically punctuate "Heart of Darkness" like a recurring leitmotif. The wilderness surrounding the Central Station, says Marlow, "struck me as something great and invincible, like evil or truth, waiting patiently for the passing away of this fantastic invasion" (76). Of that silent nocturnal wilderness Marlow asserts, "All this was great, expectant, mute, while the man [one of the agents at the station] jabbered about himself. I wondered whether the stillness on the face of the immensity looking at us two were meant as an appeal or as a menace. . . . Could we handle that dumb thing, or would it handle us? I felt how *big*, how confoundedly big, was that thing that couldn't talk and perhaps was deaf as well" (81—emphasis JHM). "It was the stillness of an implacable force brooding over an inscrutable intention. It looked at you with a vengeful aspect. . . . I felt often its mysterious stillness watching me at my monkey tricks, just as it watches you fellows [his listeners on the *Nellie*] performing on your respective tight-ropes for—what is it? half a crown a tumble—" (93–4).

The wilderness destroys Kurtz by a kind of diabolical seduction: "The wilderness had patted him on the head, and, behold, it was like a ball—an ivory ball; it had caressed him, and—lo!—he had withered; it had taken him, loved him, embraced him, got into his veins, consumed his flesh, and sealed his soul to its own by the inconceivable ceremonies of some devilish initiation. He was its spoiled and pampered favourite" (115). The Africans at Kurtz's Inner Station vanish "without any perceptible movement of retreat, as if the forest that had ejected these beings so suddenly had drawn them in again as the breath is drawn in a long aspiration" (134).

This last citation indicates another and not unpredictable feature of the *prosopopoeias* in "Heart of Darkness." The personification of the wilderness is matched by a corresponding transformation of the African people who intervene between Marlow and the "it." Just as in Thomas Hardy's *The Return of the Native* the extravagant personification of the heath in the night time that opens the novel leads to the assertion that Eustacia Vye, who rises from a mound in the heath to stand outlined in the darkness, is, so to speak, the personification of the personification, its crystallization or visible embodiment, so in "Heart of Darkness" all the Africans Marlow meets are visible representatives and symbols of that "it." Though it may be racist for Marlow (not necessarily Conrad, the reader should remember) to see the Africans as an inscrutably "other," as simple "savages" or "primitives," when their culture is older than any European one and as complex or sophisticated, if not more so, this otherness is stressed for the primary purpose of making the Africans visible embodiments and proofs that the "it," the darkness, is a person. This is an underlying feature of all Marlow's *prosopopoeias*, but it is made most explicit in the scene where Kurtz's African mistress appears on the shore:

> She was savage and superb, wild-eyed and magnificent; there was something ominous and stately in her deliberate progress. And in the hush that had fallen suddenly upon the whole sorrowful land, the immense wilderness, the colossal body of the fecund and mysterious life seemed to look at her, pensive, as though it had been looking at the image of its own tenebrous and passionate soul.... She stood looking at us without a stir, and like the wilderness itself, with an air of brooding over an inscrutable purpose. (135–6)

This passage, like the one describing the way the wilderness has seduced Kurtz, seems to indicate that this "it" is after all gendered, that it is female, a colossal body of fecund and mysterious life. Since the wilderness is supposed to represent a mysterious knowledge, "like evil or truth," this personification does not jibe very well with the "sexist" assertions Marlow makes about the way women in general are, like Kurtz's Intended, "out of *it*," invincibly innocent and ignorant. At the least one would have to say that two contradictory sexist myths about women are ascribed to Marlow, the European male's tendency to personify the earth as a great mother, full of an immemorial, seductive wisdom, and the European male's tendency to condescend to women as innately incapable of seeing into things as well as men can.

All four of these stylistic features constitute a demand that "Heart of Darkness" be read, read as literature, as opposed to being taken as a straightforwardly mimetic or referential work that would allow the reader to hold Conrad himself directly responsible for what is said as though he were a journalist or a travel writer. Of course any of these features can be used in a non-literary work, but taken all together they invite the reader to declare, "This is literature."

In the name of just what higher responsibility does Conrad justify all this indirection and ironic undercutting, suspending, or redirecting of the straightforwardly mimetic aspect of his novella? In the name of what higher obligation is everything that is referentially named in a pseudo-historical or mimetic way displaced by these ubiquitous rhetorical devices and made into a sign for something else? If "Heart of Darkness" is a literary work rather than history or autobiography, just what kind of literary work is it, just what kind of apocalypse? What lies behind that veil?

The frame narrator, in a passage often cited and commented on, gives the reader a precious clue to an answer to these questions, though it is left to the reader to make use of the clue in his or her reading:

> The yarns of seamen have a direct simplicity, the whole meaning of which lies within the shell of a cracked nut. But Marlow was not typical (if his propensity to spin yarns be excepted), and to him the meaning of an episode was not inside like kernel but outside [the Ms has "outside in the unseen"], enveloping the tale which brought it out only as a glow brings out a haze, in the likeness of one of those misty halos that sometimes are made visible by the spectral illumination of moonshine. (48)

"To spin yarns" is a cliché for narration. To tell a story is to join many threads together to make a continuous line leading from here to there. Of that yarn cloth may be woven, the whole cloth of the truth as opposed to a lie that, as the proverbial saying has it, is "made up out of whole cloth," a cloth making a web, screen, or veil covering the truth that remains hidden behind or within.

This inside/outside opposition governs the narrator's distinction between two kinds of tales. The first is the sort of seaman's yarn it was assumed by many readers and critics Conrad was telling in his stories and novels. Its meaning lies within, like the shell of a cracked nut. I take it this names a realistic, mimetic, referential tale with an obvious point and moral. Marlow's tales, on the other hand, and, by implication at least, this one by Conrad, since so much of it is made up of Marlow's narration, have a different way of making meaning. All the visible, representational elements, all that the tale makes you see, according to that famous claim by Conrad that his goal was "above all to make you *see*," are there not for their own sakes, as mimetically valuable and verifiable, for example for the sake of giving the reader information about imperialism in the Belgian Congo. Those elements have as their function to make something else visible, what the manuscript calls the "unseen," perhaps even the unseeable, as the dark matter of the universe or the putative black holes at the center of galaxies can in principle never be seen, only inferred. Conrad's figure is a different one from those black holes about which he could not have known, though it is still an astronomical trope. It is an example of that peculiar sort of figure that can be called a figure of figure or a figure of figuration. Just as the mist on a dark night is invisible except when it is made visible as a circular halo around moonlight, light already secondary and reflected from the sun, and just as the mimetic elements of Marlow's tale are secondary to the real things they represent at one remove, so the meaning of Marlow's yarns is invisible in itself and never named in itself. It is not inside the tale but outside, "brought out" indirectly by the things that are named and recounted, thereby made visible, just as, for example, Marlow when he visits the Intended hears Kurtz's last words breathed in a whisper by the dusk: "The dusk was repeating them in a persistent whisper all around us, in a whisper that seemed to swell menacingly like the first whisper of a rising wind. 'The horror! The horror!'" (149). The reader will note the way the whispered sound is onomatopoeically echoed here in the repetition three times of the word "whisper," with its aspirant and sibilant "whuh" and "isp" sounds. The illumination provided by the tale is "spectral." It turns everything into a ghostly phantom, that is, into something that is a revenant, something that has come back from the dead, and that cannot die, that will always, sooner or later, just when we least expect it, come again. The miniature lesson in aesthetic theory the frame narrator presents here is an admirably succinct distinction between mimetic literature and apocalyptic, parabolic, or allegorical literature. In the latter everything named, with however much verisimilitude, stands for something else that is not named directly, that cannot be named directly, that can only be inferred by those that have eyes to see and ears to hear and understand, as Jesus puts it in the parable of the sower in Matthew 13. All these genres have to do with the promise, with death, with the truly secret, and with last things, "things," as Jesus says, "which have been kept secret from the foundation of the world" (Matthew, 13: 35). It is not so absurd as it might seem to claim that "Heart of Darkness" is a secular version of what are (originally at least) intertwined religious or sacred genres: apocalypse, parable, allegory. Conrad himself spoke of the "piety" of his approach to writing and of his motive as quasi-religious. "One thing that I am certain of," he wrote in a letter to Arthur Symons, "is that I have approached the object of my task, things human, in a spirit of piety. The earth is a temple where there is going on a mystery play childish and poignant, ridiculous and awful enough in all conscience. Once in I've tried to behave decently. I have not degraded the quasi-religious sentiment by tears and groans; and if I have been amused or indignant, I've neither grinned nor gnashed my teeth" (CL, IV, 113).

In the case of "Heart of Darkness" just what is that "something else" for the revelation of which the whole story is written? The clear answer is that the something else is that "it" that Marlow's narration so persistently personifies and that Kurtz passes judgment on when he says "The horror! The horror!" Everything in the whole story, all the mimetic and very similar elements, is for the sake of bringing out a glimpse of that "it," the revelation of which is promised by the frame narrator when he defines the characteristic indirection of meaning in Marlow's yarns.

Many critics, perhaps even most critics, of "Heart of Darkness" have made the fundamental mistake of taking the story as an example of the first kind of seaman's yarn. That is certainly the way Achebe reads it. Those critics, like F. R. Leavis, who have noticed all the language about the "unspeakable" and "inscrutable" "it" have almost universally condemned it as so much moonshine interfering with Conrad's gift for making you see, his gift for descriptive vividness. At least such critics have taken the trouble to read carefully and have noticed that there are important verbal elements in the text that must be accounted for somehow and that do not fit the straightforward mimetic, descriptive paradigm.

Is the "something," the "it," revealed, brought into the open where it may be seen and judged? The clear answer is that it is not. The "it" remains to the end "unnamable," "inscrutable," "unspeakable," falsely, or at any rate unprovably, personified as having consciousness and intention by Marlow's rhetoric, named only indirectly and inadequately by all those similes and figures of veils being lifted. How could something be revealed that can only be revealed to those who have crossed over the threshold of death? The reader is told that "it" is "The horror! The horror!" but just what that means is never explained except in hints and indirections. Nothing definite can be said of the "it" except that it is not nothing, that it is, though even that is not certain, since it may be a projection, not a solicitation, call, or demand from something wholly other. Of the "it" one must say what Wallace Stevens says of the "primitive like an orb," "at the center on the horizon": "It is and it / Is not and, therefore, is." If "it" is wholly other it is wholly other, and nothing more can be said of it except by signs that confess in their proffering to their inadequacy. Each veil lifts to reveal another veil behind.

The structure of "Heart of Darkness" is the structure of the endlessly deferred promise, the implicit promise that Marlow makes at the beginning of his tale when he says that though his meeting with Kurtz, "the farthest point of navigation and the culminating point of my experience," was "not very clear," nevertheless "it seemed to throw a kind of light" (51). Marlow promises to pass this light or illumination on to his hearers. The primary narrator passes it on to us, the readers. The fulfillment of this promise to reveal, however, remains always future, something yet to come, eschatological or messianic rather than teleological. It is an end that can never come within the conditions of the series of episodes that reaches out towards it as life reaches towards death, or as Revelations promises an imminent messianic coming that always remains future, to come, but only beyond the last in the series, across the threshold into another realm and another regime. It is *in* the name of this unrevealed and unrevealable secret, out of obligation to it, *in* response to the demand it makes, while still remaining secret and inaccessible, that all "Heart of Darkness" is written. The presence within the novella of this inaccessible secret, a secret that nevertheless incites to narration, is what makes it appropriate to speak of "Heart of Darkness" as literature.

The place where this ultimate failure of revelation is made most explicit is Marlow's comment on the difference between Kurtz, who summed up at the moment of his death, giving words to "the appalling face of a glimpsed truth" (151), and his own illness that took him to the brink of death and then back into life again, therefore not quite far enough to see what Kurtz saw:

> And it *is* not my own extremity I remember best—a vision of greyness without form filled with physical pain, and a careless contempt for the evanescence of all things—even of this pain itself. No! It is his extremity that I seemed to have lived through. True, he had made that last stride, he had stepped over the edge, while I had been permitted to draw back my hesitating foot. And perhaps in this is the whole difference; perhaps all the wisdom, and all truth, and all sincerity, are just compressed into that inappreciable moment of time in which we step over the threshold of the invisible. Perhaps! (151—emphasis JHM)

How would one know without crossing that bourne from which no traveler ever returns? If you know you are, necessarily, no longer around to tell the tale. Even knowing this remains, necessarily, a matter of "perhaps."

It is, however, *in* the name of this non-revelation, this indirect glimpse, as the moon spectrally illuminates a ring of mist, that Marlow's judgment of imperialism is made. The "it" is the black back-cloth before which all the serio-comic antics of those carrying on the merry dance of death and trade, including their racism and sexism, are ironically suspended, made to appear both horrible and futile at once. The ubiquity of the "it" allows Marlow to imply the identity between Kurtz's African mistress and his Intended that is so crucial to the story, as well as to assert an all-important identity between the early Roman conquerors of Britain, present-day British commerce as represented by the Director of Companies, the Lawyer, and the Accountant, and the enterprise of imperialism in Africa. Of the Eldorado Exploring Expedition, Marlow says, "To tear treasure out of the bowels of the land was their desire, with no more moral purpose at the back of it than there is in burglars breaking into a safe" (87).

The same thing, however, is said about the Romans near the beginning of Marlow's narration in a way that gives it universal application: "The conquest of the earth, which mostly means the taking it away from those who have a different complexion or slightly flatter noses than ourselves, is not a pretty thing when you look into it too much" (50–1). "Heart of Darkness" looks into it. It was seen by early readers as an unequivocal condemnation of Leopold II and of Belgian imperialism in the Congo. I note in passing that now (1998) that a new regime has taken over in the Congo, transnational companies are fighting for the rights to exploit mineral deposits there, for example copper. The new global economy is not all that different from the imperialism of Conrad's day. It is not surprising that the novella represents in Marlow Eurocentric views. It was written by a European. Nor is it surprising that it represents sexist views, however much those are to be deplored. It was written to dramatize the views of an imaginary protagonist, a white male of Conrad's class and time, just as Conrad's critics represent their times, races, sexes, and nations. I claim, however, that by being displaced into Marlow as narrator and by being measured against the "it" these views are radically criticized and shown as what they are, that is, as elements in a deadly and unjust ideology.

What of Kurtz, however? Is he not different from the other agents of imperialism, who are possessed by "a flabby, pretending, weak-eyed devil of a rapacious and pitiless folly" (65). They have no insight into the way they are victims of the imperialist ideology as well as victimizers of those it exploits. Kurtz, however, "was a remarkable man," as Marlow himself repeatedly asserts, in a phrase he picks up from one of the agents. On the one hand the story of Kurtz's degradation is the familiar narrative cliché of the European who "goes native." Kurtz, like Lingard, Lord Jim, and even Charles Gould, in other novels by Conrad, crosses over a border, ceases to be European, sets himself up as a sort of King in the alien land, thereby anticipating the destiny of most colonies to become ultimately independent nations and thereby betray in one way or another ideals, the ethos, the laws and conventions, of the colonizing country. The United States did that in 1776. The somewhat ludicrous fear that this will happen, or that it will necessarily be a disaster if it does happen, has haunted the colonial enterprise from the beginning. On the other hand Kurtz never completely makes that break. After all, he allows Marlow to rescue him when he has crawled back ashore to join the Africans who have become his subjects. He dies oriented toward Europe and toward the hope that he will "have kings meet him at railway stations on his return from some ghastly nowhere, where he intended to accomplish great things" (148).

The reader will perhaps have foreseen the conclusion toward which my evidence is drawing me. The complex contradictory structure of Kurtz's ideology of imperialism repeats exactly the complex ideology that sees a literary work as the apocalyptic promise of a never-quite-yet-occurring revelation. It would not be a promise if it were not possible that the promise might not be kept. The literary promise of an always postponed revelation is strikingly exemplified not only by Marlow's narration but also by "Heart of Darkness" as a whole. Conrad's work, not just Marlow's fictive work, fits this paradigm. This makes a chain of spectral duplications that is already prepared by formal and figural features I have described.

But just how does Kurtz's ideology repeat that of Marlow and of Conrad? The literary work, for example "Heart of Darkness" or Marlow's narration within it, is governed by what Derrida calls "the exemplary secret of literature,"[4] that is the endlessly deferred promise of a definitive revelation that never occurs. This structure is not only literary but also linguistic. It depends, I mean, on the fact that a work of literature is made of language and not of any other material or substance. Marlow stresses over and over that though Kurtz was a universal genius, an artist, musician, journalist, politician, and so on, his chief characteristic was his gift of language: "A voice! a voice! It was grave, profound, vibrating, while the man did not seem capable of a whisper. . . . Kurtz discoursed. A voice! A voice! It rang deep to the very last. It survived his strength to hide in the magnificent folds of eloquence the barren darkness of his heart" (135, 147). Kurtz, in short, has a magnificent mastery of language that is similar to Marlow's own, or to Conrad's. "An appeal to me in this fiendish row—is there? Very well; I hear; I admit, but I have a voice too, and for good or evil mine is the speech that cannot be silenced" (97).

What does Kurtz talk or write about?

The reader is told of the lofty idealism of the pamphlet on "The Suppression of Savage Customs." He has bewitched the particoloured Russian, as Marlow ironically attests, by "splendid monologues on, what was it? on love, justice, conduct of life—or what not" (132). Most of all, however, Kurtz's discourse is dominated by unfulfilled and perhaps unfulfillable promises made to the whole world on behalf of Eurocentric imperialist capitalism and in support of his role as its embodiment. "All Europe contributed to the making of Kurtz" (117). Kurtz is like a John the Baptist announcing the new capitalist messiah, or perhaps himself that messiah. That Kurtz's betrothed is called "the Intended" is the emblem of this future-oriented, proleptic feature of Kurtz's eloquence. "I had immense plans," he "mutters," when Marlow is trying to persuade him come back to the boat. "I was on the threshold of great things" (143). Later, as he lies dying on the ship that is taking him back toward Europe, his "discourse" is all future-oriented, all promises of great things to come: "The wastes of his weary brain were haunted by shadowy images now— images of wealth and fame revolving round his inextinguishable gift of noble and lofty expression. My Intended! my station, my career, my ideas—these were the subject for the occasional utterances of elevated sentiments" (147). The fulfillment of these promises is cut short by a death that seals a secret or "mystery" that Kurtz carries with him to the grave and that is the necessary accompaniment of his grandiose promises. In being inhabited by this mystery Kurtz is the embodiment not just of the ideology of European capitalist imperialism but of its dark shadow, a ghost that cannot be laid, the "it" that is the inescapable accompaniment of imperialism and that Marlow identifies, in figure, with both Kurtz and with the "wilderness" that has invaded his soul. Since Kurtz embodies the darkness it is logical or inevitable that he himself should become the "god" that the Africans worship and crawl before, in striking anticipation of the fascist or violent authoritarian possibilities within capitalist imperialism. Kurtz's soul, like the "it," was "an inconceivable mystery" (145). He has "a smile of indefinable meaning" (146). "His was an impenetrable darkness" (149). Marlow's allegiance to Kurtz buries him "in a vast grave full of unspeakable secrets" (138), just as Kurtz's African mistress matches the wilderness in having "an air of brooding over an inscrutable purpose" (136), an "air of hidden knowledge, of patient expectation, of unapproachable silence" (129). It was "the stillness of an implacable force brooding over an inscrutable intention" (93). Kurtz is no more able to remove the last veil in an ultimate revelation than Marlow or Conrad can in their narrations. In all three cases a promise is made whose fulfillment or definitive non-fulfillment always remains yet to come.

What can one say to explain this contradiction, that Kurtz's magnificent idealistic eloquence is at the same time inhabited by an impenetrable darkness? Both Marlow's narration and Kurtz's eloquence, since both are based on that special speech act called a promise, are subject to two ineluctable features of any promise: 1) A promise would not be a promise but rather a constative fore-knowledge if it were not possible that it will not be kept. A possible non-fulfillment is an inalienable structural feature of any promise, whether that promise is made in literature or in politics. 2) Any promise is an invocation of an unknown and unknowable future, of a secret other that remains secret and is invited to come into that hollow uncertainty of the promise. In the case of Marlow's narration, which I am taking as an exemplary literary work, what enters the narration is all that talk of the inscrutable, the impenetrable mystery, the unspeakable secret, and so on that has so offended some of Conrad's readers. In Kurtz's case, the millennial promise made by imperialist capitalism, since it is hollow at the core, cannot be separated from the possibility or perhaps even the necessity of invasion by the "it," what Conrad calls the "Heart of Darkness." Kurtz's case is exemplary of that, a parable or allegory of that necessity. No imperialist capitalism without the darkness. They go together. Nor has that spectral accompaniment of capitalism's millennial promise of world-wide peace, prosperity, and universal democracy by any means disappeared today, when the imperialist exploitation of Conrad's day and its accompanying philanthropic idealism has been replaced by the utopian promises made for the new global economy and the new regime of scientifico-bio-medico-techno-mediatic-telecommunications. As Jacques Derrida and Werner Hamacher have recognized,[5] the political left and the political right are consonant in the promises they make. The promise of universal prosperity made for the new scientific economy dominated by technology and transformative communications techniques echoes the messianic promise, a messianism without messiah, of classical Marxism. It also echoes the promise made by right-wing ideologies, even the most unspeakably brutal, for example the Nazi promise of a thousand-year Reich.

We are inundated, swamped, engulfed every day by the present form of those promises, in all the media, in newspapers and magazines, on television, in advertising, on the Internet, in political and policy pronouncements—all guaranteeing that everything will get bigger, faster, better, more "user-friendly," and lead to worldwide millennial prosperity. These promises are all made by language or other signs, "the gift of expression, the bewildering, the illuminating, the most exalted and the most contemptible, the pulsating stream of light, or the deceitful flow from the heart of an impenetrable darkness" (113–4).

I return to my beginning. Should we, ought we, to read "Heart of Darkness?" Each reader must decide that for himself or herself. There are certainly ways to read "Heart of Darkness" that might do harm, for example if it is read as straightforwardly endorsing Eurocentric, racist and sexist ideologies. If it is read, however, as I believe it should be read, as a powerful exemplary revelation of the ideology of capitalist imperialism, including its racism and sexism, as that ideology is consonant with a certain definition of literature that is its concomitant, including a non-revelatory revelation or invocation in both of an "exemplary" non-revealable secret, then, I declare, "Heart of Darkness" should be read, ought to be read. There is an obligation to do so.

NOTES

1. The "original" (but what is more problematic than this concept of an original base for a fictional work?) of the framing scene was, if Ford Madox Ford is to be believed, Conrad's residence in Stamford-le-Hope in Essex from September 1896 to September 1898. There he knew various businessmen who did indeed take weekend cruises on a yawl. "[H]e was still quivering," says Ford, "with his attempt, with the aid of the Director, the Lawyer, and the Accountant, to float a diamond mine in South Africa. For Conrad had his adventures of that sort, too—adventures ending naturally in frustration . . . while waiting for that financial flotation to mature, he floated physically during week-ends in the company of those financiers on the bosom of that tranquil waterway [the Thames]" (Ford Madox Ford, "The Setting," in Joseph Conrad, *"Heart of Darkness." An Authoritative Text, Backgrounds and Sources, Essays in Criticism*, ed. Robert Kimbrough, (New York: Norton, 1963), 127; Norton Critical Edition). "To float a diamond mine in South Africa!" Nothing is said about this in the story itself, and Marlow, the reader must always remember, must be kept strictly separate from Conrad himself, as separate as the narrator of "The Secret Sharer" must be kept from his ghostly double. Ford's testimony, however, shows that Conrad himself was complicit, or wanted to be complicit, if he could have raised the money for it, in an exploitative imperialist enterprise that is not so different from Leopold II's merciless and murderous exploitation of the Congo or from Kurtz's raiding the country for ivory. Conrad appears momentarily to have fancied himself a miniature Cecil Rhodes.

2. These citations are from the valuable "Critical History" in Joseph Conrad, *"Heart of Darkness,"* ed. Ross C. Murfin, 2nd ed. (Boston–New York: Bedford Books of St. Martin's Press, 1966), 107, 109; Bedford Case Studies.

3. Edward Said, *Culture and Imperialism* (New York: Vintage Books, 1994), 30.

4. Jacques Derrida, *Passions*, trans. David Wood, *On the Name*, ed. Thomas Dutoit (Stanford: Stanford U.P., 1995), 29.

5. Jacques Derrida, *Specters of Marx*, trans. Peggy Kamuf (New York and London: Routledge), and Werner Hamacher, *"Lingua Amissa*: The Messianism of Commodity-Language and Derrida's Specters of Marx," forthcoming from Verso in a volume of essays about Derrida's *Specters of Marx*.

BERNARD J. PARIS

The Journey to the Inner Station

As cognitive scientists have observed, we all have an elaborate theory of the world in our heads in terms of which we process our experience. It is profoundly disturbing to have that theory challenged, to encounter phenomena which it does not enable us to comprehend. Such an encounter may give rise to what Camus describes as the sentiment of the absurd. Our deepest desire, says Camus, is for familiarity and clarity, for a world in which we feel at home and that makes sense in human terms. Every culture provides such a world, creating an illusion of knowledge and permitting its members to live with realities a recognition of which would upset their whole lives: "So long as the mind keeps silent in the motionless world of its hopes, everything is reflected and arranged in the unity of its nostalgia. But with the first move this world cracks and tumbles" and we "must despair of ever reconstructing the familiar, calm surface which would give us peace of heart" (Camus 1960, 14).

This is a good description, I think, of what happens to Marlow when he goes to the Congo. His world cracks and tumbles as he encounters realities for which he is unprepared; and his conceptions of civilization, of human and physical nature, and of himself are overthrown. He experiences the anguish of alienation, incomprehension, and disenchantment as he "stands face to face with the irrational" (Camus 1960, 21). The absurd is born, says Camus, of the confrontation between the human need for clarity and "the unreasonable

From *Conrad's Charlie Marlow: A New Approach to "Heart of Darkness" and* Lord Jim: 19–36. © 2005 by Bernard J. Paris.

silence of the world." The collapse of Marlow's mental universe occurs in stages. It begins as soon as he arrives at the coast of Africa and intensifies as his journey proceeds. He develops various strategies to cope with his distress, both while he is in the Congo and after his return.

There are two Marlows in "Heart of Darkness," as there were in "Youth"—Marlow the actor who is the subject of the tale and the older Marlow who narrates it. I shall focus first on Marlow the actor, on the stages of his transformative experience, and then on the effects of this experience as they are manifested in Marlow the narrator—in his motives for telling his story, his behavior toward his auditors, and his efforts to make sense of what has happened, to cope with the blows he has received, and to construct a mental universe in which he can live.

* * *

When he journeys to Africa, Marlow leaves a familiar environment that makes sense to him and enters a world which becomes increasingly alien and unintelligible. Before he even reaches the Congo, he experiences a sense of bewilderment that is a foretaste of what is to come. The French steamer on which he is traveling keeps landing customhouse officers in what looks "like a God-forsaken wilderness, with a tin shed and a flagpole lost in it" (505). What are customhouses doing in such places? The ship lands not only officials but also soldiers to take care of them, some of whom, he hears, are drowned in the surf as they try to reach shore. Whether they are drowned or not, nobody seems "particularly to care. They were just flung out there, and on we went." Marlow feels that he is witnessing a "sordid farce," that he is kept "away from the truth of things, within the toil of a mournful and senseless delusion."

It is not Africa by which Marlow is bewildered and appalled but the behavior of his fellow Europeans. He expects their actions to make sense, and when they do not, he feels that he is losing touch with reality. The surf seems natural, as does the appearance of boats paddled by natives, who, unlike the soldiers and customs officials, want "no excuse for being there" (506). Marlow finds the boats "a great comfort to look at. For a time I would feel I belonged still to a world of straightforward facts." By "straightforward facts" he means, of course, phenomena that his theory of the world has led him to anticipate and has made intelligible. He is prepared for the natives, but quite unprepared for the sight of a French man-of-war shelling the bush, where there isn't even a shed in sight: "In the empty immensity of earth, sky, and water, there she was, incomprehensible, firing into a continent." The six-inch guns go "pop," but nothing happens: "Nothing could happen. There was a touch of insanity in the proceeding."

Compounding Marlow's sense of the insanity of the proceeding is his learning that men on the gunboat are "dying of fever at the rate of three a day" (506). In the world in which he has lived, life is regarded as precious; and when death comes, it is surrounded by ceremony and managed in ways that give it a special dignity. Here, however, death is treated casually and has become commonplace and routine. If soldiers drown in the surf, nobody seems to care, and the ship sails on. If men on the gunboat are dying of fever while it futilely shells the bush, no one seems to care about that either.

Talking about lies later on, Marlow says that there is "a taint of death, a flavor of mortality" in them, "which is exactly what I hate and detest in the world—what I want to forget" (526). This passage is usually cited in connection with Marlow's lie to the Intended, but is also important for his attitude toward death. Death is one of the realities Camus had in mind, the recognition of which would upset our whole lives. In his trip on the French steamer, Marlow begins to confront death without the cultural trappings that conceal its brute reality and help to keep at bay the sentiment of the absurd which arises when we realize how incompatible with human desire the order of things really is. He had sloughed off the intimations of death he encountered in Brussels, but he can do so no longer, and he now sees death everywhere. The steamer calls at "more places with farcical names" (farcical because unfamiliar), "where the merry dance of death and trade goes on in a still and earthly atmosphere of an overheated catacomb" (507).

The "sense of vague and oppressive wonder" (507) that grows on Marlow as the steamer approaches the mouth of the Congo is intensified when he reaches the "scene of inhabited devastation" (508) that constitutes the company station. Instruments of civilization are there but in complete disarray. A boiler is wallowing in the grass, a railway truck is lying with its wheels in the air, and imported drainage pipes, all of them broken, have been tumbled into a ravine. The Europeans are ostensibly building a railway, but they are accomplishing nothing and their behavior cannot be explained. They are dynamiting a cliff that is not in the way, and the "objectless blasting" produces no change in the rock, much as the gunboat firing pointlessly into the continent has no effect on the wilderness. Marlow encounters "a vast artificial hole somebody had been digging on the slope," the purpose of which he finds it "impossible to divine" (510). It isn't a quarry or a sandpit; it is "just a hole" to which no meaning can be attached. Everything in the station is "in a muddle" (513), and human activities partake of the absurd.

The only exception is the chief accountant, whom Marlow sometimes visits "to be out of the chaos" (513). He is elegantly dressed and keeps his books in good order, accomplishments Marlow respects considering "the great demoralization of the land" (512). He keeps up his morale by teaching one of the native women to care for his linen, thus reinstituting his familiar world.

His "starched collars and got-up shirt fronts are achievements of character," says Marlow. The accountant's sense of what constitutes civilized behavior is very narrow, however; and he can maintain his sense of order only by being insensitive to what is transpiring around him, including the suffering of his fellow human beings. He hates the clamor of the savages and complains that the groans of an expiring agent distract his attention, making correct entries difficult. Like the men on the French steamer, he seems indifferent to the scenes of mortality by which he is surrounded. While the sick agent is "lying flushed and insensible," the accountant, "bent over his books," is "making correct entries of perfectly correct transactions" (514). From his doorstep, Marlow can see the "grove of death."

In Marlow's view, of course, the transactions are far from perfectly correct. Marlow had dismissed the humbug about "weaning those ignorant millions from their horrid ways," and had hinted to his aunt "that the company was run for profit" (504). But he had not expected the brutal exploitation of the natives he encounters in the Congo. The categories used by the Europeans to justify their behavior seem ridiculous under the circumstances. The natives being shelled by the gunboat are "enemies," and those in the chain gang at the company station are "criminals," to whom "the outraged law, like the bursting shells, had come ... an insoluble mystery" (509). In an African setting European civilization has turned into something bizarre; and Marlow identifies with the natives, who are also suffering from the unfamiliarity and unintelligibility of the world into which they have been transported. Brought from their homes "in all the legality of time contracts" they do not understand, and "lost in uncongenial surroundings," they become profoundly disoriented. They sicken, become inefficient, and are allowed to crawl away and die. It is these natives who inhabit the "grove of death" that is visible from the accountant's doorstep. The correctness of the company's transactions is maintained by imposing the illusion of legality on behavior that fills Marlow with horror. He cannot help feeling some guilt, for he is "after all ... a part of the great cause of these high and just proceedings."

The 200-mile trek to the Central Station deepens Marlow's sense of the disorder into which the Europeans have fallen and the chaos they have brought to the land. In response to their fellows having been caught and forced to carry loads for the white men, the native people have cleared out, and the villages are empty and desolate. Again, Marlow identifies with the natives, imagining what the reaction would be at home if a lot of mysterious marauders "armed with all kinds of fearful weapons" took to raiding the countryside (515). He recognizes that the drums he hears in the distance might have a meaning, like the sound of bells in a Christian country, whereas the behavior of the Europeans seems incomprehensible. He encounters a white man accompanied by an armed escort, who declares that he is "looking after the upkeep of the road." The discovery of a negro with a bullet hole in his forehead three miles farther on makes a mockery of this claim. Marlow wonders if the corpse is to be considered "a permanent improvement." Exasperated by his overweight companion who keeps fainting from the heat, falls ill, and needs to be carried by the porters, Marlow asks him what he means "by coming there at all" (516). "To make money, of course," is the reply. Driven by their rapacity, the white men are careless not only of the lives of others but of their own lives as well.

As a result of his experiences so far, Marlow feels himself undergoing an internal transformation. He remembers the old doctor in Brussels: "'It would be interesting for science to watch the mental changes of individuals on the spot.' I felt I was becoming scientifically interesting" (516).

The fragility of civilization and its liability to collapse are on full display at the Central Station. The steamer Marlow has come to command has been foolishly wrecked, and it seems impossible to obtain the rivets needed for its repair. Rivets were strewn about in great abundance at the first station, where they were put to no use; but all that can be obtained from that station is a stream of trashy merchandise to be employed in bartering for ivory. When a hut full of this merchandise catches on fire, a man assures Marlow that everyone is behaving splendidly as he scoops a quart of water from the river into a pail with a hole in its bottom. Marlow had received a similar assurance about everyone's behavior when the steamer was sunk. There is a brickmaker who, for lack of an essential ingredient, has not been able to make bricks. There are the plotting agents ("the pilgrims") who make a "philanthropic pretense" and a "show of work" while being motivated solely by greed and never lifting a finger effectually (522).

The collapse of civilized values is most clearly evident, perhaps, in the station's manager and his uncle, the leader of the Eldorado Exploring Expedition. The manager does not have the courtesy to ask Marlow to sit after his twenty-mile hike that morning, but this is a small thing. He has achieved his position of authority despite the fact that he has no learning, no intelligence, no initiative, and no organizational ability, as "the deplorable state of the station" testifies (518). What he has is "triumphant health in the general rout of constitutions." While those around him sicken and die, he is never ill. His power derives from his animal health and his amorality, from the fact that he is one of the hollow men. As various tropical diseases lay low his agents, he observes that "men who come out here should have no entrails." He inspires not respect but unease: "He was great by this little thing that it was impossible to tell what could control such a man. He never gave that secret away. Perhaps there was nothing within him. Such a suspicion made one pause—for out there there were no external checks."

The manager's uncle is similarly devoid of scruples. The members of the Eldorado Exploring Expedition are "sordid buccaneers" whose desire "to tear treasure out of the bowels of the land" has "no more moral purpose at the back of it than there is in burglars breaking into a safe" (531–32). When the manager complains of a wandering trader who has been obtaining ivory from the natives, his uncle urges him to have the fellow hanged as an example: "Why not? Anything—anything can be done in this country" (534). Both men are scornful of Kurtz, who had preached that "each station should be like a beacon on the road toward better things, a center for trade of course, but also for humanizing, improving, instructing" (535). "Conceive you," the manager exclaims, "that ass!" The uncle urges his nephew to trust for his ultimate triumph to "the lurking death" that is carrying off everyone else.

Overhearing this "treacherous appeal" to the "hidden evil" of the land, Marlow is so appalled that he leaps to his feet, as though he expects "an answer of some sort to that black display of confidence" (535). He encounters instead the "high stillness" of the wilderness, what Camus would call the unreasonable silence of the universe. His sense of order is somewhat restored when he later learns that the Expedition's donkeys are all dead: "I know nothing of the fate of the less valuable animals. They, no doubt, like the rest of us, found what they deserved" (536). Despite being elegantly equipped, the reckless and greedy buccaneers lack "foresight" and "serious intention," not seeming to be aware that "these things are wanted for the work of the world" (531). They perish for want of the civilized virtues that are necessary when confronting the forces of nature.

It is at the Central Station that Marlow becomes more vividly aware of these forces—their magnitude, their unconsciousness, their unresponsiveness to human beings. In civilization the natural world has been humanized and subdued, so that its otherness and unruliness have been concealed. Marlow's Congo experience makes him aware of realities that have been hidden from him before: the fragility of civilization, the moral and physical weakness of European man, and the power of nature, which makes a mockery of human pretensions of mastery. The "silent wilderness surrounding this cleared speck on the earth," strikes him "as something great and invincible . . . waiting patiently for the passing away of this fantastic invasion" (520). In Europe, human efforts to master the physical universe seem triumphant. In the Congo, "the great wall of vegetation" is "like a rioting invasion of soundless life, a rolling wave of plants" ready "to sweep every little man of us out of his little existence" (530–31). Marlow is being forced to see himself and his fellows in relation not to the human community, in which they feel protected and at home, but to a natural world in which they are insignificant and radically insecure.

It is at the Central Station also that Marlow begins to develop his defenses against the threatening experiences he is undergoing. One of his defenses is to turn his back on the station and go to work: "In that way only it seemed to me I could keep my hold on the redeeming facts of life" (520). By repairing the steamer he is undoing the folly that had led to its being wrecked, he is restoring one of the instruments by which civilized man asserts his will in a natural environment, and he is insulating himself from the inefficiency, disorder, and turpitude that have overtaken his fellow Europeans. He is creating a physical and mental space within which his theory of the world can be maintained. In addition, as he says a bit later, he is finding himself—his own reality, which is that of a man who has the discipline, knowledge, and foresight which are necessary for survival in an inhospitable universe.

Marlow's other principal defense is to hold himself morally aloof from the behavior of the white men, to remain true to his training and principles. Although much of what is going on around him is so disorganized and counterproductive that it does not make sense to him, he is never in doubt as to the immorality of the deeds being perpetrated in the name of the "great cause." His need to dissociate himself from "these high and just proceedings" leads him to be severely judgmental. His outrage, horror, and scorn are affirmations of the values that seem to have collapsed in the face of temptation and greed. Despite the general demoralization, civilization still has a champion in Marlow.

Marlow becomes interested in Kurtz because he has the impression that Kurtz is also a champion of civilization. The brickmaker tells him that Kurtz is "an emissary of pity, and science, and progress" (523) who has been sent to the Congo by "the gang of virtue," those who believe in the company's mission as an agent of progress. Because of Kurtz's success as chief of the Inner Station, there is a fear that he might gain further promotion and be in a position to interfere with the exploitation of the natives. The brickmaker has the impression that Marlow is also of the "new gang" (524) and that he therefore has influence in Europe. Marlow allows him to imagine anything he likes as to his influence, although this comes close to telling a lie, because he thinks it might somehow be of help to Kurtz. His sense of alliance with Kurtz is strengthened when he overhears the manager indignantly complain to his uncle of "the pestiferous absurdity" of Kurtz's talk about each station's being "a beacon on the road toward better things" (535). He is "curious to see whether this man who had come out equipped with moral ideas" would rise to the top and "how he would set about his work" (532). In Kurtz he hopes to find evidence that civilization can triumph in the wilderness and that not all white men are like those he has encountered so far. Once the steamboat is repaired and begins its trip to the Inner Station, it crawls "exclusively," for Marlow, "towards Kurtz" (538).

* * *

The journey up the Congo deepens Marlow's awareness of the untamed in nature and the primitive in man. Going up the river is "like traveling back to the earliest beginning of the world, when vegetation rioted on the earth and the big trees were kings" (536). This "prehistoric world" wears "the aspect of an unknown planet" (539). Marlow is encountering the planet as it was before human activity transformed it into the familiar place in which he has felt at home. "We are accustomed to look upon the shackled form of a conquered monster," he tells his auditors, but here nature is "monstrous and free" (539– 40). Marlow finds this experience profoundly unsettling. Instead of feeling that he lives in a relatively safe and manageable universe, which is responsive to human needs, he finds himself in an eerily silent world that has the aspect of "an implacable force brooding over an inscrutable intention" (537). Nature, not man, is in control; and although its ways cannot be fathomed, it seems inimical to human beings (537).

As Marlow penetrates more deeply into the wilderness, the disorientation from which he has been suffering is intensified. The strangeness of the setting makes the earth appear "unearthly" (539), whereas the shackled monster to which he was accustomed had seemed natural and real. And yet, "this strange world of plants, and water, and silence" has an "overwhelming reality" that makes everything one has known seem like "an unrestful and noisy dream" (536). Marlow feels at once "cut off forever" from his past and unable to comprehend his present surroundings, which are menacing and inscrutable.

As had been the case at the Central Station, Marlow is saved by the necessities of work, in this case of navigation. He has to keep guessing at the channel, watching out for snags, hidden banks, and sunken stones. As a result, he does not see the ominous world around him any more: "When you have to attend to . . . the mere incidents of the surface, the reality—the reality, I tell you, fades. The inner truth is hidden—luckily, luckily" (537). Nonetheless, he still feels the "mysterious stillness" watching him at his "monkey tricks, just as it watches" his auditors performing on their "respective tightropes for—what is it? A half crown a tumble—." When one of his listeners objects to Marlow's incivility, he retreats: "indeed, what does the price matter, if the trick be well done? You do your tricks very well. And I didn't do badly either, since I managed not to sink that steamboat on my first trip."

We see here in Marlow the narrator an oscillation between cosmic and communal perspectives that begins to develop while he is in the Congo. From the cosmic perspective—which sees human activities against the backdrop of a vast, uncaring, unintelligible universe—our endeavors are just a bunch of monkey tricks that have no meaning in a larger scheme of things. The objectives we strive for and anguish over are unimportant, and it does not greatly matter what we do. While he is arguing with himself as to whether he should talk openly about company affairs when he meets Kurtz, it occurs to Marlow that his speech or his silence, indeed any action of his, "would be a mere futility. What did it matter what anyone knew or ignored? What did it matter who was manager? One gets sometimes such a flash of insight" (544). One of the major effects of his Congo experience on Marlow is that the communal perspective he brings with him is challenged by the breakdown of civilized order and restraint amongst the white men and his encounter with nature as a monster unshackled and free. His previous values, concerns, and beliefs seem unreal, with no grounding in the larger universe; and human activities seem futile and pointless.

Although at times the communal perspective seems to be swallowed up by the cosmic, there are also occasions on which it is reaffirmed. One such occasion is when Marlow finds a copy of *An Inquiry into Some Points of Seamanship*, a book that had been left behind in his former dwelling by the young Russian. This is not an enthralling book, but its "honest concern for the right way of going to work" in its treatment of technical matters such as purchases and chains makes Marlow "forget the jungle and the pilgrims in a delicious sensation of having come upon something unmistakably real" (543). When he must stop reading in order to continue his journey, it is like "tearing [himself] away from the shelter of an old and solid friendship." This is something more than escaping the disturbing realities of the cosmic process by attending to incidents of the surface; it is an affirmation of another, competing truth that is equally real.

The book is representative of the community by which Marlow has been sheltered, of the techniques by which human beings have learned to manage the forces of nature and impose their will on the world. From the cosmic perspective, these techniques may be seen as monkey tricks; but when they are well done, they succeed; and their success is not insignificant to those who perform them. Marlow does his tricks well; for, despite all the hazards, he does not sink the boat. The steamer is "like a sluggish beetle crawling on the floor of a lofty portico. It made you feel very small, very lost, and yet it was not altogether depressing, that feeling. After all, if you were small, the grimy beetle crawled on—which was just what you wanted it to" (538). This passage reflects both the cosmic and communal perspectives, each of which has its validity.

Marlow's trip up the Congo takes him more deeply not only into the alien world of unshackled nature but also into the nature of human beings. It is a journey backward in time, to an early stage in social development; and it is also a journey within, to what lies buried beneath the surface in civilized men. Marlow learns that although we appear to have moved far beyond our prehistoric origins, we are subject to atavistic regression when we are taken out of our cultural setting and external supports are removed. He encounters various stages of decivilization as he journeys first on the French steamer to Africa and then to the company stations, with Kurtz being, as we shall see, the most extreme example of the primitive behavior of which Europeans are capable.

Marlow also encounters natives in various stages of transition, and he is sensitive to the effect on them, as well as on the white men, of being removed from the physical and cultural environments into which they were born. He can empathize with the "workers" and "criminals" at the first company station and with the native members of his crew on the steamer, including the cannibals who mysteriously refrain from eating the white men, even though they are starving because they have not been provided with food.

The most primitive of the natives are those Marlow observes on the banks of the river as the steamer is passing by. At first he finds their frenzy "incomprehensible." The Europeans are "secretly appalled, as sane men would be before an enthusiastic outbreak in a madhouse. We could not understand because we were too far and could not remember, because we were traveling in the night of first ages, of those ages that were gone, leaving hardly a sign—and no memories" (539). It slowly dawns on him, however, that the savages are "not inhuman" and that he feels a "remote kinship with this wild and passionate uproar" (540). He finds in himself "just the faintest trace of a response to the terrible frankness of that noise, a dim suspicion of there being a meaning in it" that he can comprehend. He cannot precisely identify the emotions being expressed, but he recognizes them as akin to his own: "What was there after all? Joy, fear, sorrow, devotion, valor, rage—who can tell?—but truth—truth stripped of its cloak of time." The emotions are like those of civilized men, but their expression is far less inhibited.

As he does with unshackled nature, Marlow sees in unrestrained humans the hidden truth that lies beneath the veneer of civilization, the truth that seems to be emerging in the atavistic behavior of the Europeans and in his own dim response to the wild and passionate uproar on the riverbank. He didn't "go ashore for a howl and a dance" (540), he tells his auditors, partly because he was preoccupied with bandaging leaky steam pipes, watching the steering, and circumventing snags, and partly because of an "inborn strength" that enabled him to resist the "appeal" of "this fiendish row." Marlow's invocation of "inborn strength" suggests that his Congo experience puts him in touch not only with primitive forces that lie deep in human nature but also with something equally hidden and true that has the ability to resist those forces. Just as the techniques of civilization are as unmistakably real as the power of nature, so in human beings there can be a capacity for restraint that is just as intrinsic as the impulses toward selfishness, greed, and aggression.

Marlow says that in order to look on "truth stripped of its cloak of time" "without a wink," a man "must meet that truth with his own true stuff—with his own inborn strength" (540). I do not believe that this passage, and others like it, has been well-understood in Conrad criticism.

Marlow, like Conrad, is a neo-Lamarckian who believes in the biological inheritance of acquired characteristics. Such a belief was widespread in the nineteenth and the first half of the twentieth centuries. In *Experiments in Life: George Eliot's Quest for Values* (1965), I discussed its presence in George Eliot, Herbert Spencer, G. H. Lewes, and Charles Darwin. This belief resulted in the placing of various races or nationalities along an evolutionary scale, from the most primitive to the most civilized—a practice that justified the domination of ostensibly inferior peoples in the process of economic exploitation and political empire-building (see Hruska 1975) and that resulted in such horrors as the Nazi ideology.

Marlow is opposed to the Europeans' treatment of native populations, but he sees the Africans as representative of an earlier stage of human evolution. They have, for example, no "clear idea of time, as we at the end of countless ages have. They still belonged to the beginnings of time—had no inherited experience to teach them as it were" (547). This is a neo-Lamarckian conception of where categories of perception, such as time, originate. They are not a priori, as idealistic philosophers contend, but are products of the experience of past generations and the resulting modifications of structure, which are biologically transmitted to their posterity. Although the categories may be inborn and a priori for individuals, they did not precede the experience of the species. The cannibals of whom Marlow is speaking are at such an early stage of evolution that they have not yet developed a clear idea of time.

In the system of beliefs to which Marlow seems to subscribe, there arises out of the unconscious, amoral cosmic process a human order that generates values, techniques, and social organizations that stand in opposition to the blind ways of nature. The law of the cosmic process is the survival of the fittest, whereas that of the human order is the fitting of as many as possible to survive. To succeed, the human order requires discipline and restraint, the shackling not only of the monstrous world of external nature but also of the brute instincts within. Civilized human beings are the product both of the cosmic process, which is still very much alive in their depths, and of their socialization and training, which places the good of the community above their selfish and anarchic impulses and leads them to transcend their primitive instincts. Societies support the restraints they require in many ways—through various external sanctions, such as laws, police, and public opinion; through moral and religious indoctrination; and through divisions of labor that create specialized groups to butcher animals, fight wars, and do other dirty work. What Marlow is discovering, to his dismay, in the Congo is how readily civilized men revert to the primitive when such supports are removed.

Civilized values are transmitted and enforced not only by social institutions but also through the inheritance of acquired moral predispositions. People are not born with an articulated moral code but with an innate receptiveness to the values of their culture that is the biological counterpart of social institutions. The social and biological embodiments of racial experience reinforce each other, with the biological predispositions leading individuals to perceive the codes of their culture as inwardly dictated absolutes. The strength of people's organic morality is tested when external constraints are removed and there is nothing but their "innate strength" (560), their "true stuff" (540), to keep their primitive impulses under control.

In this neo-Lamarckian scheme, each race or nationality (the terms were often used interchangeably) has its own cultural history and biological inheritance. Innate discipline and moral predispositions are better and stronger in some than in others. This helps us to understand a passage in "Youth" that provides crucial insights into Marlow's racial attitudes. After the *Judea* blows up, the maddened Captain Beard orders the men to go aloft and furl the sails. This act is both pointless and dangerous, since the ship is "doomed to arrive nowhere" and the masts may topple over at any moment (139). The men do it, nevertheless, and they do it very carefully, under the leadership of the romantic young Marlow, who is consciously thinking "how fine" it is (140). The older, narrating Marlow asks what made them do it, what made the men follow his orders when he insisted that they "drop the bunt of the foresail twice to try and do it better." They were a bunch of Liverpool scalawags "without the drilled-in habit of obedience." It wasn't professional pride, a sense of duty, or the pay that motivated them:

> No; it was something in them, something inborn and subtle and everlasting. I don't say positively that the crew of a French or German merchantman wouldn't have done it, but I doubt whether it would have been done in the same way. There was a completeness in it, something solid like a principle, and masterful like an instinct—a disclosure of something secret of that hidden something, that gift of good or evil that makes racial difference, that shapes the fate of nations. (140)

Through the inheritance of acquired characteristics, principles have become like instincts, operating masterfully in the absence of external inducements and constraints.

There is a great difference for Marlow not only between savages living in the night of first ages and civilized men who are products of a lengthy evolutionary process, but also between the various European nationalities. When he looks at the map of Africa in the company's office in Brussels, he sees a great many colors, each signifying the colonizing power. Among the colors, there is "a vast amount of red [for England]—good to see at any time, because one knows that some real work is done in there"—presumably unlike the purple "where the jolly pioneers of progress drink the jolly lager beer" (500). It is important to note that in Marlow's tale the men who regress under the influence of Africa are Belgian or French, or of mixed nationality. The British Marlow is somewhat tempted but not seduced by the call of the wild.

Marlow's conception of human nature helps us to understand not only what he means by "innate strength" (560) but also what is missing in the men he characterizes as hollow, such as the manager of the Central Station and the brickmaker, whom he describes as a "papier-mâché Mephistopheles": "it seemed to me that if I tried I could poke my forefinger through him, and would find nothing inside but a little loose dirt, perhaps" (525). When he reaches the Inner Station, he finds a genuine Mephistopheles, a man who shows what can happen when there are neither external restraints nor internal ones.

Chronology

1857	Józef Teodor Konrad Korzeniowski born December 3 in Berdyczew, Poland, to Apollo Korzeniowski and Ewelina Bobrowska.
1862	Joseph Conrad's father is exiled to Russia for his part in the Polish National Committee. Conrad and his mother accompany his father.
1865	Mother dies.
1869	Conrad and his father return to Krakow in February. Father dies in May.
1874	Leaves Krakow for Marseilles, intending to become a sailor.
1875	Becomes apprentice aboard the *Mont Blanc*, bound for Martinique.
1877	Part owner of the *Tremolino*.
1878	In February, after ending an unhappy love affair, Conrad attempts suicide by shooting himself. In June, he lands in England. Serves as ordinary seaman on the *Mavis*.
1883	Becomes mate on the ship *Riversdale*.
1884	Second mate on the *Narcissus*, bound from Bombay to Dunkirk.
1886	Becomes naturalized British citizen.
1887	First mate on the *Highland Forest*.

1889	Begins writing *Almayer's Folly*.
1890	In May, leaves for the Congo as second in command of the S. S. *Roi de Belges*, later becoming commander.
1894	Ends sea career.
1895	Publishes *Almayer's Folly*. Writes *An Outcast of the Islands*. Lives in London.
1896	Marries Jessie George on March 24.
1897–1900	Writes *The Nigger of the "Narcissus," Heart of Darkness*, and *Lord Jim*.
1904	Writes *Nostromo*.
1905	Travels in Europe for four months.
1907	Writes *The Secret Agent*.
1911–12	Writes *Under Western Eyes* and *'Twixt Land and Sea*.
1914	Writes *Chance* and *Victory*. In July, visits Poland, where he is caught when World War I breaks out in August. Escapes and returns safely to England in November.
1916	Son, Borys, fights on the French front.
1917	Writes *The Shadow-Line* and prefaces to an edition of his collected works.
1919	Writes *The Arrow of Gold*.
1920	Writes *The Rescue*.
1924	In May, declines a knighthood. After an illness, dies of a heart attack on August 3 and is buried in Canterbury.
1925	The incomplete *Suspense* is published. *Tales of Hearsay* is published.
1926	*Last Essays* published.

Contributors

HAROLD BLOOM is Sterling Professor of the Humanities at Yale University. He is the author of 30 books, including *Shelley's Mythmaking, The Visionary Company, Blake's Apocalypse, Yeats, A Map of Misreading, Kabbalah and Criticism, Agon: Toward a Theory of Revisionism, The American Religion, The Western Canon,* and *Omens of Millennium: The Gnosis of Angels, Dreams, and Resurrection. The Anxiety of Influence* sets forth Professor Bloom's provocative theory of the literary relationships between the great writers and their predecessors. His most recent books include *Shakespeare: The Invention of the Human,* a 1998 National Book Award finalist, *How to Read and Why, Genius: A Mosaic of One Hundred Exemplary Creative Minds, Hamlet: Poem Unlimited, Where Shall Wisdom Be Found?,* and *Jesus and Yahweh: The Names Divine.* In 1999, Professor Bloom received the prestigious American Academy of Arts and Letters Gold Medal for Criticism. He has also received the International Prize of Catalonia, the Alfonso Reyes Prize of Mexico, and the Hans Christian Andersen Bicentennial Prize of Denmark.

EDWARD W. SAID was a professor at Columbia University. He wrote or edited many titles, including *Joseph Conrad and the Fiction of Autobiography* and *Orientalism.*

CEDRIC WATTS is a professor at the University of Sussex. He has written several titles on Conrad, such as *Joseph Conrad: A Literary Life* and *A Preface to Conrad.* Also, he has edited a number of Conrad's works and written on other authors as well.

JOHN G. PETERS is an associate professor at the University of North Texas. He is the author of *Conrad and Impressionism* and *The Cambridge Introduction to Joseph Conrad*. He has written and translated other works as well.

PERICLES LEWIS is an associate professor at Yale University. He is the author of *Modernism, Nationalism, and the Novel* and is working on *Religious Experience in the Modern Novel* and *The Cambridge Introduction to Modernism*.

HANS ULRICH SEEBER is a professor emeritus at the University of Stuttgart. He is an editor of *Magic, Science, Technology and Literature*.

JAMES MORGAN is an associate professor at the Massachusetts Maritime Academy.

PADMINI MONGIA is a professor of English at Franklin and Marshall College and has been chair of the English department there as well. Aside from her work on Conrad, she is working on *Indo Chic: Marketing English India*.

J. HILLIS MILLER is Distinguished Research Professor at the University of California, Irvine. Some of his works are *Charles Dickens: The World of His Novels* and *Poets of Reality*.

BERNARD J. PARIS is a University of Florida professor emeritus. He has written many books, including *A Psychological Approach to Fiction: Studies in Thackeray, Stendhal, George Eliot, Dostoevsky, and Conrad*.

Bibliography

Atkinson, William. "Bound in Blackwood's: The Imperialism of the *Heart of Darkness* in Its Immediate Context." *Twentieth Century Literature: A Scholarly and Critical Journal* 50, no. 4 (Winter 2004): 368–93.

Baldridge, Cates. "Joseph Conrad's *Heart of Darkness*." In *British Writers: Classics*, volume one, edited by Jay Parini, 123–40. New York: Scribner's, 2003.

Barnett, Clive. "'A Choice of Nightmares': Narration and Desire in *Heart of Darkness*." *Gender, Place & Culture* 3, no. 3 (1996): 277–91.

Billy, Ted. "Heart of Darkness (1899).'" In *A Joseph Conrad Companion*, edited by Leonard Orr and Ted Billy, 65–78. Westport, Conn.: Greenwood, 1999.

Caminero-Santangelo, Byron. *African Fiction and Joseph Conrad: Reading Postcolonial Intertextuality*. Albany: State University of New York Press, 2005.

Carabine, Keith, ed. *Joseph Conrad: Critical Assessments*, four volumes. Sussex: Helm Information, 1992.

Chon, Sooyoung. "Writing as an Exodus from Two Empires." In *Under Postcolonial Eyes: Joseph Conrad After Empire*, edited by Gail Fincham and Myrtle Hooper. Cape Town: University of Cape Town Press, 1996.

Cole, Sarah. "Conradian Alienation and Imperial Intimacy." *MFS: Modern Fiction Studies* 44, no. 2 (Summer 1998): 251–81.

Cousineau, Thomas. *"Heart of Darkness*: The Outsider Demystified." *Conradiana: A Journal of Joseph Conrad Studies* 30, no. 2 (Summer 1998): 140–51.

De Lange, Attie, Gail Fincham, and Wieslaw Krajka. *Conrad in Africa: New Essays on Heart of Darkness*. Boulder, Colo., and Lublin, Poland: Social Science Monograph and Maria Curie-Sklodowska University, 2001.

Devlin, Kimberly J. "The Scopic Drive and Visual Projection in *Heart of Darkness*." *MFS: Modern Fiction Studies* 52, no. 1 (Spring 2006): 19–41.

Dong, Lan. "Countervailing Movements of Time and Space: Narrative Structure of *Heart of Darkness*." *Interactions: Aegean Journal of English and American Studies* 15, no. 1 (Spring 2006): 65–75.

Dryden, Linda J. "'To Boldly Go': Conrad's *Heart of Darkness* and Popular Culture." *Conradiana: A Journal of Joseph Conrad Studies* 34, no. 3 (Fall 2002): 149–70.

Erdinast-Vulcan, Daphna. "*Heart of Darkness* and the Ends of Man." *Conradian: Journal of the Joseph Conrad Society* 28, no. 1 (Spring 2003): 17–33.

Firchow, Peter Edgerly. *Envisioning Africa: Racism and Imperialism in Conrad's* Heart of Darkness. Lexington, Ky.: University Press of Kentucky, 2000.

Fleming, Bruce E. "Brothers Under the Skin: Achebe on *Heart of Darkness*." *College Literature* 19/20 (October 1992/February 1993): 90–9.

Galef, David. "On the Margin: The Peripheral Characters in Conrad's *Heart of Darkness*." *Journal of Modern Literature* 17, no. 1 (1990): 117–38.

Gibson, Andrew. "Ethics and Unrepresentability in *Heart of Darkness*." *Conradian: Journal of the Joseph Conrad Society* 22, nos. 1–2 (Spring–Winter 1997): 113–37.

Gogwilt, Christopher. *Joseph Conrad and the Invention of the West*. Stanford: Stanford University Press, 1995.

Hampson, Robert. "*Heart of Darkness* and 'The Speech that Cannot Be Silenced.'" *English: Journal of the English Association* 39, no. 163 (Spring 1990): 15–32.

Hawkins, Hunt and Brian W. Shaffer, eds. *Approaches to Teaching Conrad's* Heart of Darkness *and "The Secret Sharer."* New York: Modern Language Association of America, 2002.

Kaplan, Carola M. "Colonizers, Cannibals, and the Horror of Good Intentions in Joseph Conrad's *Heart of Darkness*." *Studies in Short Fiction* 34, no. 3 (Summer 1997): 323–33.

Kim, Chang-hyun. "Interaction of the Realistic and the Mythic Structure in Conrad's *Heart of Darkness.*" *Journal of English Language and Literature* 48, no. 4 (Winter 2002): 901–13.

Kim, Jong-Seok. "Bewildered Encounters in Conrad's *Heart of Darkness.*" *Studies in Modern Fiction* 8, no. 2 (Winter 2001): 285–312.

Kimmel, Michael. "From Metaphor to the 'Mental Sketchpad': Literary Macrostructure and Compound Image Schemas in *Heart of Darkness.*" *Metaphor and Symbol* 20, no. 3 (2005): 199–238.

Lee, Man-sik. "The Implicit Writer in *Heart of Darkness.*" *Nineteenth-Century Literature in English* 10, no. 1 (2006): 205–23.

Lothe, Jakob. "The Problem of Narrative Beginnings: Joseph Conrad's *Heart of Darkness* and Francis Ford Coppola's *Apocalypse Now.*" *Revue des Lettres Modernes: Histoire des Idées et des Littératures* 1286-4633 (2002): 35–58.

McIntire, Gabrielle. "The Women Do Not Travel: Gender, Difference, and Incommensurability in Conrad's *Heart of Darkness.*" *MFS: Modern Fiction Studies* 48, no. 2 (Summer 2002): 257–84.

Miller, J. Hillis. "*Heart of Darkness* Revisited." In *Tropes, Parables, Performatives: Essays on Twentieth-Century Literature,* 181–94. London: Harvester Wheatsheaf, 1990.

Moore, Gene M., ed. *Joseph Conrad's* Heart of Darkness: *A Casebook.* Oxford, England: Oxford University Press, 2004.

Myers, Jeffrey. "The Anxiety of Confluence: Evolution, Ecology, and Imperialism in Conrad's *Heart of Darkness.*" *Isle: Interdisciplinary Studies in Literature and Environment* 8, no. 2 (Summer 2001): 97–108.

Nazareth, Peter. "Dark Heart or Trickster?" *Nineteenth-Century Literature in English* 9, no. 3 (2005): 291–321.

Paccaud-Huguet, Josiane. "'One of Those Trifles That Awaken Ideas': The Conradian Moment." *Conradian: Journal of the Joseph Conrad Society* 31, no. 1 (Spring 2006): 72–85.

_____. "The Remains of Kurtz's Day: Joseph Conrad and Historical Correctness." *Conradiana: A Journal of Joseph Conrad Studies* 36, no. 3 (Fall 2004): 167–84.

Parras, John. "Poetic Prose and Imperialism: The Ideology of Form in Joseph Conrad's *Heart of Darkness.*" *Nebula* 3, no. 1 (April 2006): 85–102.

Parry, Benita. "The Moment and Afterlife of *Heart of Darkness.*" In *Conrad in the Twenty-First Century: Contemporary Approaches and Perspectives,* edited by Carola M. Kaplan, Peter Lancelot Mallios, and Andrea White, 39-53. New York: Routledge, 2005.

Prescott, Lynda. "*Heart of Darkness*: Plots, Parallels and Post-Colonialism." In *The Nineteenth-Century Novel: Identities*, edited by Dennis Walder, 311–30. London, England: Open University Press and Routledge, 2001.

_____. "Joseph Conrad and the Imperial Vision: *Heart of Darkness*." In *The Nineteenth-Century Novel: Identities*, edited by Dennis Walder, 287–310. London, England: Open University Press and Routledge, 2001.

Ross, Stephen. "Desire in *Heart of Darkness*." *Conradiana: A Journal of Joseph Conrad Studies* 36, nos. 1–2 (Spring–Summer 2004): 65–91.

Rozema, David L. "Faith in the *Heart of Darkness*: What Conrad Intended with 'the Intended.'" *Christian Scholar's Review* 29, no. 2 (Winter 1999): 303–21.

Schnauder, Ludwig. "Marlow's Journey in Conrad's *Heart of Darkness*: Crisscrossing the Boundaries of Imperialist Ideology and Epistemology." *eSharp: Electronic Social Sciences, Humanities, and Arts Review for Postgraduates* 4 (Spring 2005): 1–12.

Schneider, Lissa. "Iconography and the Feminine Ideal." In *Joseph Conrad* Heart of Darkness: *Authoritative Text, Backgrounds and Contexts Criticism*, edited by Paul Armstrong, 474–83. New York: Norton, 2006.

Skinner, John. "From Modernism to Postcolonialism: Shifting Perspectives on Conrad's *Heart of Darkness*." In *Approaches to Narrative Fiction*, edited by Jon Buscall and Outi Pickering, 51–66. Turku, Finland: University of Turku, 1999.

Stampfl, Barry. "Marlowe's Rhetoric of (Self-) Deception in *Heart of Darkness*." *MFS: Modern Fiction Studies* 37, no. 2 (1991): 183–96.

Stape, J. H. "'The Dark Places of the Earth': Text and Context in *Heart of Darkness*." *Conradian: Journal of the Joseph Conrad Society* 29, no. 1 (Spring 2004): 144–61.

Stape, J. H., and Owen Knowles. "Marlow's Audience in 'Youth' and *Heart of Darkness*: A Historical Note." *Conradian: Journal of the Joseph Conrad Society* 31, no. 1 (Spring 2006): 105–16.

Swisher, Clarice, ed. *Readings on* Heart of Darkness. San Diego, Calif.: Greenhaven, 1999.

Tredell, Nicolas. *Joseph Conrad:* Heart of Darkness. New York: Columbia University Press, 1998.

Trench-Bonett, Dorothy. "Naming and Silence: A Study of Language and the Other in Conrad's *Heart of Darkness*." *Conradiana: A Journal of Joseph Conrad Studies* 32, no. 2 (Summer 2000): 84–95.

Watts, Cedric. "'A Bloody Racist': About Achebe's View of Conrad." In *Joseph Conrad: Critical Assessments*, edited by Keith Carabine, 405–18. Sussex: Helm Information, 1992.

White, Andrea. "Conrad and Imperialism." In *The Cambridge Companion to Joseph Conrad*, edited by J. H. Stape. Cambridge: Cambridge University Press, 1996.

Wilson, Donald S. "The Beast in the Congo: How Victorian Homophobia Inflects Marlow's *Heart of Darkness*." *Conradiana: A Journal of Joseph Conrad Studies* 32, no. 2 (Summer 2000): 96–118.

Acknowledgments

Edward W. Said, "Two Visions in *Heart of Darkness,*" *Culture and Imperialism.* Copyright © 1993 by Edward W. Said, reprinted with permission of The Wylie Agency, Inc.

Cedric Watts, "*Heart of Darkness,*" *The Cambridge Companion to Joseph Conrad.* Reprinted by permission of Cambridge University Press.

John G. Peters, "The Opaque and The Clear: The White Fog Incident in Conrad's 'Heart of Darkness,'" *Studies in Short Fiction* 35, 1998.

Pericles Lewis "'His Sympathies Were in the Right Place': *Heart of Darkness* and the Discourse of National Character," *Nineteenth-Century Literature,* vol. 53, no. 2, September 1998.

Hans Ulrich Seeber, "Surface as Suggestive Energy. Fascination and Voice in Conrad's 'Heart of Darkness,'" *Joseph Conrad: East European, Polish and Worldwide.* Boulder, CO: East European Monographs, 1999.

James Morgan, "Harlequin in Hell: Marlow and the Russian Sailor in Conrad's Heart of Darkness," *Conradiana,* Spring 2001, vol. 33, no. 1. © 2001 Texas Tech University Press, 2001, 1-800-832-4042.

Padmini Mongia, "The Resuce: Conrad, Achebe, and the Critics," *Conradiana,* vol. 33, no. 2, 2001. © 2001 Texas Tech University Press, 2001, 1-800-832-4042.

J. Hillis Miller, "Should We Read 'Heart of Darkness,'" *Conrad in Africa: New Essays on "Heart of Darkness,"* Boulder, CO: Social Science Monographs, 2002.

Bernard J. Paris, "The Journey to the Inner Station," *Conrad's Charlie Marlow: A New Approach to "Heart of Darkness" and* Lord Jim, Palgrave Macmillan, 2005. Reprinted by permission.

Every effort has been made to contact the owners of copyrighted material and secure copyright permission. Articles appearing in this volume generally appear much as they did in their original publication with few or no editorial changes. In some cases, foreign language text has been removed from the original essay. Those interested in locating the original source will find the information cited above.

Index